CHILDREN'S ENGLISH AND SERVICES STUDY

LANGUAGE MINORITY CHILDREN WITH LIMITED ENGLISH PROFICIENCY IN THE UNITED STATES

J. Michael O'Malley

ACKNOWLEDGMENTS

This study represents a striking example of successful collaboration among Federal agencies and of cooperation between Federal and State agencies concerned with education research and language minority issues. The study was largely funded by the National Institute of Education with a contribution from the National Center for Education Statistics, and with additional contributions from the U.S. Office of Bilingual Education and the Assistant Secretary for Planning and Evaluation in the Department of Health, Education, and Welfare. State Education Agencies contributed staff time to advise the Federal agencies on the design of essential components of the study. The study was monitored by NIE with technical assistance from NCES. Comments and suggestions on the draft reports were provided by the Interagency Part C Committee on Bilingual Research, and the results of the household survey were reviewed under contract with NCES.

For their contributions to the development and design of the study, the following individuals must be acknowledged. Leslie Silverman of NCES was a continual source of energy and of confidence that imposing technical obstacles could be overcome, while often indicating the path which led to their solution. His colleague at NCES, Dorothy Waggoner, was a strong contributor to the design stage of the study through her familiarity with language surveys and bilingual education. The Chief State School Officers of many (roughly 30) States freed time for their senior staff to serve on a review team for the study. Some of those staff who contributed most heavily, particularly to the design of the language instrument, were José Martínez of California, Ernest Mazzone of Massachusetts, María Ramírez of New York, Elena Vergara of Indiana, and Robin Johnston of Colorado.

This list of acknowledgments would not be complete without a sincere expression of gratitude to the participating language minority children and their families and to the schools in which the children were enrolled.

This document is published by InterAmerica Research Associates, Inc., pursuant to contract NIE 400-80-0040 to operate the National Clearinghouse for Bilingual Education. The National Clearinghouse for Bilingual Education is jointly funded by the National Institute of Education and the Office of Bilingual Education and Minority Languages Affairs, U.S. Department of Education. Contractors undertaking such projects under government sponsorship are encouraged to express their judgment freely in professional and technical matters; the views expressed in this publication do not necessarily reflect the views of the sponsoring agencies.

InterAmerica Research Associates, Inc. d/b/a
National Clearinghouse for Bilingual Education
1300 Wilson Boulevard, Suite B2-11
Rosslyn, Virginia 22209
(703) 522-0710 / (800) 336-4560

ISBN: 0-89763-057-2
First printing 1981
Printed in USA

10   9   8   7   6   5   4   3   2   1

CONTENTS

LIST OF TABLES

EXECUTIVE SUMMARY

LANGUAGE MINORITY CHILDREN WITH LIMITED ENGLISH PROFICIENCY IN THE UNITED STATES

SPRING 1978

An estimated 2.4 million children with limited English language proficiency aged 5-14 years were living in the United States in the Spring of 1978. This number represents 63% of all children aged 5-14 years living in households where a language other than English was spoken. In addition, there were estimated to be as many as 1.2 million limited English proficient children younger or older than the 5-14 year olds but also of school age. The number of limited English proficient children aged 5-14 was estimated from the first study of its scope ever conducted in the United States to determine the number of language minority children with limited English proficiency.

Limited English language proficiency was found to be more prevalent among children living in households where Spanish was spoken and among children in three major states as contrasted with the remainder of the country. However, limited English proficiency did not differ markedly by age. The findings are discussed in detail below.

RESULTS BY LANGUAGE

More children aged 5-14 years living in households where Spanish was spoken were limited in English proficiency compared to children of the same age living in households where other non-English languages were spoken.

- There were 1.7 million Spanish language background children aged 5-14 years with limited english proficiency. This was 73% of the total number of children in this age range living in households where Spanish was spoken.

- There were .7 million children aged 5-14 years from all other language minority backgrounds combined with limited English proficiency. This was 47% of the total number of children in this age range living in households where other non-English languages were spoken.

RESULTS BY AGE

The percentage of limited English proficient children among all children living in households where a language other than English was spoken did not differ markedly by age. The following percentages are for various age groups, for all languages combined:

5-6 year olds:	67% limited in English
7-8 year olds:	68% limited in English
9-11 year olds:	59% limited in English
12-14 year olds:	61% limited in English

RESULTS BY STATE

An estimated 1.5 million or 62% of all limited English proficient children lived in three states: California, Texas, and New York. The figures by state are as follows for all languages combined:

California	594,000 limited in English
New York	468,000 limited in English
Texas	438,000 limited in English
Remainder of U.S.	908,000 limited in English
Total	2,408,000 limited in English

New York had the highest percentage of children who were limited in English proficiency among children aged 5-14 years living in households where a language other than English was spoken. The figures are:

New York	77% limited in English
California	70% limited in English
Texas	70% limited in English
Remainder of U.S.	53% limited in English
Total	63% limited in English

SOURCE OF DATA

The Children's English and Services Study was conducted under contract from the National Institute of Education with shared support from the National Center for Education Statistics and the U.S. Office of Education. The study was designed to respond to a Congressional mandate in the Bilingual Education Act (Elementary and Secondary Education Act, Title VII) to count the number of children with limited English speaking ability in the United States. The work was carried out by a consortium headed by L. Miranda & Associates, Inc., of Washington, D.C. as prime contractor.[1]

Adults were interviewed in the Spring of 1978 in a nationally representative sample of approximately 35,000 households. About 2,200 households were identified where a language other than English was spoken and where children between the ages of 5 and 14 were living. Within these households, selected children were individually administered a test in English that determined whether or not the child was limited in English language proficiency. The sample was designed to provide representative numbers of children in California, Texas, New York, and the remainder of the country.

The test in English was designed to meet the definition of limited English proficiency in the Bilingual Education Act. Representatives of 30 State Education Agencies developed specifications for the test and served on a review team for the study. The reviewers found that no existing test would meet the Congressional intent. They urged development of a test measuring age-specific speaking, listening, reading, and writing skills in English. The test criterion for limited English proficiency is a cut-off point on the total score that accurately classifies children as limited or not limited in English for their age level. The criterion was derived from field work with an independent sample.

The Children's English and Services Study is one of a number of studies undertaken by the Education Division of the Department of Health, Education, and Welfare to assess educational needs and to improve instructional effectiveness for limited English proficient children.

ACCURACY OF THE DATA

Because the results are based on a sample rather than a census of the population, all figures provided in this report are estimates with an error range within which the true score may lie with a 95% level of confidence. Examples of the error range follow.

The national estimate of limited English proficient children aged 5-14 years is 2.4 million. The number 2.4 million is 63% of all children in the age range 5-14 living in households where a language other than English is spoken, with a range from 55% to 71% at a 95% level of confidence.

METHODOLOGICAL REVIEW

A methodological review of this report was prepared by the National Center for Educational Statistics (NCES), Office for Research Analysis (ORA).[2] In the review, three analytical issues were discussed:

- Were the items which were selected for inclusion in the Language Measurement and Assessment Inventory (LM&AI) selected properly?

- Were the cutoff scores for the LM&AI, which were determined and used to classify children as either English proficient or of limited English proficiency (LEP), set properly?

- What were the effects of nonresponse bias on the counts and estimates of LEP children?

Accordingly, NCES/ORA offered the following recommendations:

1. There should be a caveat concerning the limitations of the CESS results "which are a function of the current state-of-the-art in the assessment of language proficiency."[3]

2. Using an alternative analytic procedure NCES/ORA reported a 9.22% higher estimate of LEP children. Their recommendation was to include this information in the report.

3. In regard to nonresponse bias, NCES/ORA concluded "that further investigations. . .are not warranted."[4]

Issues concerning the state-of-the-art in language proficiency assessment in general are discussed in the NCES document. A response to NCES/ORA estimation procedures, however, has been prepared by the National Institute of Education (NIE).[5] The NCES/ORA review and NIE response may be accessed through the National Clearinghouse for Bilingual Education.

FOREWORD

In this work Dr. J. Michael O'Malley examines the background, rationale, procedures, and results of a study by the National Institute of Education (NIE) and the National Center for Education Statistics (NCES) to determine the number of limited English proficient children living in the United States and the types of services these children receive in school.

Dr. J. Michael O'Malley is project director for the 1980-1981 Teachers Languages Skills Survey to determine the number of teachers in the U.S. who have the appropriate language skills and background to offer instruction to limited English proficient children. The project is administered by InterAmerica Research Associates through support from the Office of Bilingual Education and Minority Languages Affairs in the U.S. Department of Education. Dr. O'Malley has been research consultant and director for various projects and evaluative studies in the areas of early childhood education, bilingual education, and youth employment. While a senior research associate at the National Institute of Education, he was project officer for the Children's English and Services Study.

One of the activities of the National Clearinghouse for Bilingual Education is to publish documents addressing the specific information needs of the bilingual education community. We are pleased to make this title available through our growing list of publications. Subsequent Clearinghouse products will similarly seek to contribute information that can assist in the education of minority language and culture groups in the United States.

National Clearinghouse
for Bilingual Education

I. INTRODUCTION

For the past several years, the Education Division in the Department of Health, Education, and Welfare has performed a series of studies to determine the educational needs of language minorities living in the United States. School age children with limited proficiency in English are of particular concern in these studies. Limited English proficient children have been the focus of Federal and State legislation in bilingual education and of a Supreme Court decision directing schools not to discriminate against national origin minority children on the basis of language proficiency.

The Education Division has attempted to answer fundamental questions through these studies about the level and types of educational services appropriate for limited English proficient children. The questions are of the following kind. First, how many children are there with limited proficiency in English? In the absence of information on the total number of children, projections to establish appropriate levels of service are mere speculation. Second, what are the educational needs of limited English proficient children? Beyond the count of children, projections of future service requirements should take into account the special needs these children may have. And finally, what types of services are required for children whose needs are not being addressed? Specific information about types of programs and staffing is required.

An important interim goal of the Education Division's studies has been achieved: a count has been completed of the number of limited English proficient children living in the United States. This report is a description of the background, rationale, procedures, and results of the study designed to produce that count.

Legislative Mandates

The count of limited English proficient students was first mandated in the Bilingual Education Act, Title VII of the Elementary and Secondary Education Act (ESEA), as amended in 1974. The count was required as part of a report on the condition of bilingual education in the nation to be submitted by the Commissioner of Education, which would include

> "A national assessment of the educational needs of children and
> other persons with limited English-speaking ability and of the
> extent to which such needs are being met by Federal, State and
> local efforts, including (A). . .the results of a survey of the
> number of such children and persons in the States, and (B) a plan,
> including cost estimates. . .for extending programs of bilingual
> education. . .to all such preschool and elementary school children
> and other persons of limited English-speaking ability. . ." Section
> 731 (c) (1)

The Congress went on to mandate the count to the National Center for Education Statistics (NCES):

> "The National Center for Education Statistics shall conduct the survey
> required by Section 731 (c) (1) (A) of Title VII of the Elementary and
> Secondary Education Act." Section 501 (b) (4)

At the same time, the Bilingual Education Act required the National Institute of Education (NIE) to "determine the basic educational needs of children with limited English speaking ability" in Section 742 (c) (1).

In combination, the Congressional mandates to identify needs and services for the Commissioner's report, the mandate for the count of limited English speaking children, and the mandated NIE activities constituted a sizeable needs assessment effort in bilingual education. The needs assessment was intended by Congress to establish the scope of bilingual education in the future and play a role in determining future funding levels.

Prior Research Efforts

Shortly after the Education Amendments of 1974 were enacted into law, NCES began a series of investigations in response to the legislative mandate for a survey of the number of language minority persons with limited English-speaking ability. A 1970 Census question on the language used in the household when a person was a child, i.e., the mother tongue, would not suffice for information on language proficiency. A strategy was needed to produce information on language proficiency in the context of a household survey. The following discussion traces the direction of the NCES investigations and their contribution to the foundation necessary to estimate numbers of limited English speaking persons.

Survey of Income and Education (SIE). The SIE was the major NCES response to the mandated survey. The SIE was required in the Education Amendments of 1974 to furnish current data on the number of school-age children in poverty for purposes of formula allocation of ESEA Title I support. By cooperative agreement with the Bureau of the Census, which conducted the SIE, NCES included language questions on the SIE household interview and supplemented the SIE sample in selected states wherever necessary to provide acceptably accurate state level estimates of language minority persons of school age. In a series of reports, NCES has indicated the geographic distribution, country of origin, and school enrollment status of language minorities based on the SIE (NCES 1978a, 1978b, 1978c, 1979). The SIE language questions concentrated on language background, usage, and English proficiency. Because detailed information on these language characteristics had not previously been collected on a national scale, extensive development work on the language questions was required to carry out the response to the mandate.

Survey of Languages. The Survey of Languages had two purposes. First, it was a pilot survey for questions on language characteristics and place of birth for the SIE; and second, it provided preliminary estimates of language background characteristics at the national level. The Survey of Languages was a supplement to the July 1975 Current Population Survey (CPS), a household survey performed monthly by the Bureau of the Census for the Department of Labor to obtain employment estimates and other information about the labor force. In the Survey of Languages, alternative interpretations of the legislative definition of "language minority" were developed and tested. Each interpretation yielded an estimate of the number of language minorities, among whom would be found persons with limited English-speaking ability. These estimates were described in the first Commissioner's *Report on The Condition of Bilingual Education in the Nation* in November 1976.

2

Measure of English Language Proficiency (MELP). In the SIE, direct assessment of the language proficiency of school-age children from language minority backgrounds was not possible. The Bureau of the Census wished to maintain a household interview format on the SIE and prohibited the use of paper and pencil tests, electronic recordings, or direct interviews of each household member in the sample. Thus, field work separate from the SIE was needed to identify a set of "census-type" questions that would predict English language proficiency as a surrogate for more thorough assessment criteria. This set of "census-type" questions constituted the MELP. In the field work, performed under contract with NCES, the assessment criteria were an English language proficiency test, direct ratings by the interviewer of the child's English language proficiency, and school district classification of language minority children as either limited or proficient in English-speaking ability. The method for predicting English language proficiency from the MELP was based on correlational techniques and procedures that maximized accurate classifications when predicting the assessment criteria. Simulations of the prediction in the field test revealed that questions on language usage and skill in speaking and understanding English were useful in the prediction. However, it was also found that the MELP items could be composed differently to produce accurate classifications depending on the proportion of limited English speaking children in the language minority group. Because the proportion was the unknown, a separate study was required for the MELP in the SIE to be useful in providing state level estimates of the number of limited English speaking children.

Children's English and Services Study

By cooperative agreement among agencies in the Education Division, the study to determine the proportion of language minority children with limited English-speaking ability was performed under contract from NIE with shared support from NCES and the U.S. Office of Education. The study was titled the Children's English and Services Study (CESS) and was contracted to a consortium headed by L. Miranda & Associates, Inc., a Washington-based consultant firm. Westat of Rockville, Maryland and Resource Department Institute of Austin, Texas were LM&A's major subcontractors in the consortium.

In addition to providing estimates of the proportion of language minority children with limited English-speaking ability, the CESS was designed to provide estimates of the number of limited English speaking children from Spanish language backgrounds and the aggregate of all other language minorities combined in major geographic sections of the U.S.

The CESS used a sample of households in which a language other than English was spoken usually or often, consistent with the CPS and SIE definitions, and obtained responses to the MELP questions for children aged 5-14 in those households. The external criterion for limited English proficiency was a specially constructed language assessment instrument.

The Congressional mandate for a count of limited English speaking children called for information that no previous investigation had attempted to produce at the national level. As a result, an entirely new methodology had to be created for the CESS in order to respond to the Congressional concerns. The problems of creating the methodology centered on three issues:

- **Defining limited English-speaking ability.** Acceptable criteria or test instruments for identifying limited English speaking children as defined in ESEA Title VII were required that could be used in a household survey;

- **Determining a criterion score.** Acceptable techniques were needed for identifying a criterion score below which all students could be accurately classified as limited English speaking; and

- **Identifying a representative sample.** A procedure was required for developing a probability sample of the population of language minority persons.

The methodology for resolving these three issues in the CESS required a high level of technical acceptability and coordination. The procedure had to be objective from a methodological standpoint and represent the best possible approach for addressing the issues. Federal and State linkages were imperative to establish a common framework generated from experience in bilingual program operation and, at the State level, from experience in counting limited English speaking students. Further, political sensitivity was required due to strong interests of advocacy groups in the bilingual program and the possible impact of the count on future funding levels. Thus, there were at least three important constituencies to whom the methodology should be acceptable: technical experts, Federal and State bilingual program staff, and language minority advocacy groups.

The methodology for the CESS was designed to meet the specifications of an advisory group composed of persons overlapping the three main constituencies. The advisory group was composed largely of individuals designated by their Chief State School Officer to represent bilingual education in their State but was also composed of individuals representing State data collection systems and language assessment in bilingual education. Up to 30 States were represented at various meetings of the advisory group. The advisory group was given full responsibility for setting technical specifications for the test, the criterion score, and the sample design. In a series of meetings each constituency in the advisory group was provided an opportunity to address one or more of the issues of concern by self-appointment to small group sessions that reported their findings for discussion in plenary sessions. Each constituency by self-assignment thereby assumed responsibility for setting technical specifications for portions of the methodology they chose to influence, and it became unnecessary in the advisory group to differentiate members as technical vs. practitioner vs. non-technical vs. advocacy. The methodology was thought most likely to be acceptable to the different constituencies if, collectively, they had designed the study. The Government and its consortium of contractors then became responsible for carrying out the study according to the technical specifications established by the advisory group.

The CESS data collection was conducted in Spring 1978, and data analyses were completed early in 1979. This report on the CESS contains a discussion of:

4

- the definition of limited English proficiency and the procedures for selecting a criterion score

- the sample selection and field data collection procedures

- the major results of the study including the count of limited English proficient children.

Comments on this report from selected members of the advisory group are contained in a final section. These individuals were asked to comment on the procedures followed in the study and on the findings.

II. DEFINING LIMITED ENGLISH PROFICIENCY

The Bilingual Education Act, as amended in 1974, called for a count of limited English speaking children and adults to be included as part of a report by the Commissioner of Education on the Condition of Bilingual Education in the Nation. The Children's English and Services Study (CESS) was contracted by the National Institute of Education as part of a coordinated Education Division effort to respond to the mandated count. An advisory group to the CESS participated actively in the design of the study.

Completion of the count required development of an acceptable definition of limited English speaking ability. This section of the report describes the framework for that definition, the advisory group reaction to the framework, their specifications for a new instrument, field test procedures in the development of the instrument, and the selection of a criterion score for identifying limited English proficient individuals.

Conceptual Framework

In developing an acceptable definition of limited English-speaking ability, three constraints were presented to the advisory group by the Government. First, the definition of limited English-speaking ability had to be consistent with the legislative definition in the Bilingual Education Act, as amended in 1974. The full definition is as follows:

> "The terms limited English-speaking ability when used with reference to an individual, means—
>
> (A)   individuals who were not born in the United States or whose native language is a language other than English; and
>
> (B)   individuals who come from environments where a language other than English is dominant,. . .and by reason thereof, have difficulty speaking and understanding instruction in the English language." Section 703 (a) (1)

The legislation clearly points to two components of limited English-speaking ability: (1) non-English language background, defined in terms of native language, country of origin, or language environment; and (2) limited ability in speaking and understanding English for purposes of profiting from instruction in English.

Language minority children, i.e., children from non-English language backgrounds, were the *base* population for estimating the number of limited English speaking children. Using language minority children as a base population rather than all school age children resolved imposing technical difficulties of estimating rare characteristics in the general population. Limited English proficiency was not expected to be so rare a characteristic among language minorities.

Methods for determining the base number of language minority children in the context of household surveys had been tested previously by the National Center for Education Statistics (NCES) in the Current Population Survey (CPS) and the Survey of Income and Education (SIE). The most accurate estimate of the base figure from which the CESS sample could be drawn, 3.8 million language minority children aged 5-14 years, had been obtained from the SIE.

The advisory group was presented the challenge of determining how limited English-speaking ability could be defined consistent with the legislative definition and used to identify children within the larger group of language minorities. NIE and NCES suggested that the definition selection should be based on a test of speaking and understanding in English, as implied in the 1974 Bilingual Education Act. English should be the exclusive criterion irrespective of the child's proficiency in the non-English language. Thus, language dominance was considered irrelevant to the definition.

The second constraint suggested by the Government was to produce a dichotomous classification for limited vs. not limited English-speaking ability. Language proficiency typically is portrayed along a continuum and is described as composed of numerous sub-skills. A dichotomous classification is inconsistent with this view. Nonetheless, from a policy viewpoint, the Congress appeared interested in a single estimate to determine the need for special services for limited English speaking children. From a practitioner's view-point, children are either eligible or not eligible for Title VII; they are either enrolled or not enrolled in the Title VII program. A dichotomous classification thus was thought to be consistent with Congressional intent and with school practice.

The third constraint was that the procedure adopted to define limited English-speaking ability had to be usable in the context of a household survey for children aged 5-14 years. A language test was to be administered either in schools to children in the sample or in homes with a minimum of burden to the respondent and to individuals in the setting.

The age limitation originated in funding constraints and the desire to limit the scope of a study attempting a new methodology.

Redefinition of the Conceptual Framework

The advisory group was asked to apply the framework in preparing specifications for an approach to define limited English-speaking ability. The advisory group accepted the framework except for one constraint. They rejected the portion of the first constraint requiring the definition to reflect skills in speaking and understanding English. In their experience, particularly those members from the State agencies, reading and writing skills were as crucial a determinant for bilingual program eligibility as speaking and under-standing English and thus should be included in the definition. Children from non-English language backgrounds who could not read or write in English were as much in need of bilingual instruction as children who were unable to speak or understand English. Read-ing and writing were seen as critical skills in English because language minorities unskilled in these areas would be at a disadvantage educationally in the absence of some form of instruc-tion beyond the regular, all-English program.

The reviewers' insistence on including reading and writing along with speaking and understanding in the definition of limited English speaking ability anticipated, by roughly one year, changes to be made in the Bilingual Education Act, as amended in 1978. Eligi-bility in the 1974 Amendments had been provided for children with limited English speaking ability (LESA) in only two skills areas: speaking and understanding. In the Educa-tion Amendments of 1978, eligibility was provided for children with limited English proficiency (LEP) in four skill areas: speaking, understanding, reading and writing. Because the definition of eligibility was changed in the study to accommodate changes yet to be made in the Act, the study became responsive to the new legislative definition. The reviewers thus prevented the study from being outdated immediately upon enactment of the changed definition of eligibility in the 1978 Amendments.

Selected members of the advisory group had previously searched available assessment instruments for a test that was designed to identify limited English proficient children in their own states. There was a ready concurrence among the reviewers that no existing instrument would meet the constraints of the study and satisfactorily identify eligible children consistent with the definition of limited English proficiency in ESEA Title VII. A new instrument should be developed, they agreed, meeting specifications they provided. Their specifications and the manner in which the specifications were carried out are discussed in the following sections:

1. *Domain-referenced content.* The content objectives of the new test were to tap skills necessary to profit from instruction in English in the areas of speaking, understanding, reading and writing. The skills were to be within the domain of skill requirements that, in the judgment of the State members of the advisory group, students are expected to perform when English is used as the medium of instruction. Subskills within each of the four major skill areas should be selected to represent curriculum content objectives in the states and to represent item content on major tests used to assess these objectives.

2. *Age Appropriate.* The content objectives for subskills areas were to be designed to be age appropriate by developing a different form of the instrument for every year of age in the 5-14 year range. Each form would concentrate on skills required to profit from instruction in English at the age level. The number of items assigned to assess each content objective in the subskill areas at each age level would be determined in advance by the advisory group to achieve a balanced representation of the objectives (Appendix A).

3. *Referenced to an Appropriate External Criterion.* The test was being developed to differentiate language minorities who were limited in English proficiency from those who could profit from instruction in English. Items under development were to be field tested with two clearly defined *criterion groups*: (a) limited English proficient children; and (b) fluent English speaking children who were clearly profiting from instruction in English.

   a. Students were to be selected from schools which in a systematic and acceptable manner performed classifications of limited English proficient and fluent English speakers. The limited English proficient group was to be selected with a combination of test criteria and teacher judgment about the student's ability to profit from instruction in English. The fluent English speaking group would be composed of students who were native English speakers and in the normal range of ability and school performance. The fluent English speaking group could serve as an unambiguous criterion

for being "able to profit from instruction in English."
Using this group would assure that the items were within
the range of ability of native English speakers who were
performing acceptably in school.

b. The advisory group further specified that item field
testing was to be performed with students from a range
of language minority backgrounds. Items would be re-
tained in the final version of the instrument if they
met the domain-referenced content specifications *and*
discriminated between the two criterion groups in
successive field tests as the items underwent revision.
Because the items would discriminate between the extreme
contrast groups, adding up the correct item responses to
produce a total score was expected to yield a bimodal
distribution in the field test sample.

4. *Location and Duration of Administration.* The advisory group
required that the test would be administered in the homes of the
children rather than in schools and would consume no more than
30 minutes on the average for administration.

5. *Selection of Criterion Score.* Selection of an approach to produce
a criterion score was to be integrated with the item selection
approach and overall test design. Items selected would discriminate
between limited English proficient and normally achieving native
English speakers but would also correlate positively with the total
score. The total score, by design, therefore became a relatively
coherent variable designed to perform a single function, to
discriminate systematically between children designated by schools
as limited in English proficiency or proficient in English.

In selecting an approach to identify the criterion score for each age form of the instrument, two considerations were essential. First, the approach should be easy to communi-
cate to a non-technical audience; and second, the approach should maximize the likelihood
of correct classifications of both limited and English proficient children in the field test.
Use of the total score alone–rather than some combination of subscores, particularly a
weighted combination–was expected to meet these two criteria. Children in the national
sample whose scores fell below the critical score were to be designated limited English proficient and those whose scores fell above this point were considered English proficient.

Field Test Procedures

The test developed to the advisory group specifications was the Language Measurement
and Assessment Inventory (LM&AI). Field tests were performed on a total of 1,378 children for three successive versions of 10 age forms of the instrument. The first field test
was on 144 children in a major urban area in the northeastern U.S. The second was with
445 children in a major urban area in the Midwest, and in two major urban areas on the
West coast. The final field test was conducted with 789 children in urban areas in the

Northwest, and in urban as well as less densely populated areas in the Southwest. Language groups with which the field tests were performed included Arabic, Chinese, Greek, Italian, Japanese, Polish, Spanish (Cuban, Mexican American, and Puerto Rican), and Vietnamese as well as native English speakers. Approximately equal numbers of limited English proficient and native English speaking children were selected at each site.

In each field test, extensive debriefing was conducted with over 100 teachers and other personnel who participated in the test administration. The debriefing concentrated on the importance of the content objectives for local practice, content validity and relevance of items to item objectives, sequence of item presentation during test administration, instructions for administration, time of administration, and the quality of examiner training procedures. Results of the debriefing and statistical analyses of the items were used in revisions of the instrument prior to each successive field test. Typically, tests were administered by local staff, substitute teachers, or consultants to local education agencies with experience in test administration.

Procedures used in field test sites to identify limited English proficient and fluent English speaking children varied depending on practices in the local education agencies within State guidelines. Sites were selected where procedures for classifying limited English proficient children were reported by State advisory group members to be based on systematic assessment and diagnosis of language minority children. Site personnel were requested to identify two groups of children in approximately equal number with balanced distribution of boys and girls. The first group was language minority children with limited English proficiency based on their inability to profit from instruction in English, as reflected in test results or judgments of school personnel. The second group consisted of fluent English speaking children who were native English speakers performing in the normal range of ability and school achievement. Native English speakers rather than language minorities rated English fluent were selected to assure unequivocally that the English proficiency of the group was adequate to assure their success in an English language program. More specifically, the fluent English speaking group was requested to be within a range of plus or minus one-half standard deviation from the mean of standardized achievement tests reflecting overall school performance or the equivalent in the judgment of school personnel. This range was selected to meet advisory member requirements for a criterion group that clearly was able to profit from instruction in English but was in the normal range of performance.

In selected cases, children administered the LM&AI in field tests were not included in the data analyses. There were two primary conditions that led to excluding cases from the analysis. First, field test cases were eliminated whenever school classification procedures seemed arbitrary or inexact upon inquiry at the school site. For example, in some instances, school personnel were unable to justify classifying a child as limited in English proficiency with reports of assessment or systematic observation. In other instances, children classified as fluent in English were found to be enrolled in compensatory education class and clearly did not meet the condition that they be profiting from instruction in English. The second primary reason for excluding cases from the analysis of field test data was incorrect administration of the LM&AI. In earlier versions of the instrument particularly, selected items with complex administration or recording instructions, which later were refined, sometimes were incorrectly administered.

Final Field Test Results

The purpose of the final field test was twofold: (1) to complete final item selection and revision while establishing the reliability of the overall instrument; and (2) to select a criterion score for identifying limited English proficient children.

The sample size in the third field test was reduced by 12% from 789 to 691 cases due to improper or suspect classifications and errors in test administration. The reliabilities (coefficient alpha) of the 10 age forms computed on these cases ranged from .86 to .92. The reliabilities were considered more than adequate for use of the instrument in the context of a survey where judgments affecting the educational placement of individual children were not involved. Additional information, including specific item objectives and means and standard deviations of the final test forms, is presented in Appendix A accompanied by a discussion of the purposes for which the test was designed and the limitations on its use in other contexts.

Selection of the Criterion Score

Selection of a criterion score for differentiating native English speakers from children with limited English proficiency in the third field test relied upon a discriminant function approach. The procedure is fully objective and precludes the possibility of arbitrary selection of a criterion. In using the discriminant function, one or more variables are used to predict membership in one of two groups. Group membership is the criterion. In the CESS, the predictor was the continuous score on the English language instrument administered in the third field test, and the criterion was the school designation as limited or fluent in English. The discriminant function maximizes the overall number of accurate classifications. Correctly classifying fluent English speaking children was given as much weight as correctly classifying children who were limited in English.

Accurate classifications in predicting the criterion occured when a child was classified by both the predictor and criterion as limited in English, or when a child was classified by both the predictor and criterion as fluent in English. The sum of the number of accurate classifications divided by the total number of cases across sites in the third field test provided the overall accuracy rate at each age level. The overall accuracy rate range from 82.9% to 97.2%, depending on the age form of the test. The accuracy was increased only slightly by using scores on the four subskill areas as predictors in comparison to the total score alone. Scores on the subscore areas, by design, were highly intercorrelated. Only the total score therefore was used for classifications in the national sample because the accuracy added from the subscores was negligible. Detailed information on the selection of the criterion score is included in Appendix A.

III. CONCEPTUAL FRAMEWORK AND SURVEY PROCEDURES FOR ESTIMATING NUMBERS OF LIMITED ENGLISH PROFICIENT CHILDREN

The Children's English and Service Study (CESS) was designed to portray characteristics of limited English speaking students to respond to a Congressionally mandated needs assessment in bilingual education. No prior national survey had attempted to identify or collect data on a special purpose sample of language minorities. The only prior experience was from efforts by the National Center for Education Statistics (NCES) to identify language minorities in the context of other surveys. Completion of the CESS therefore required novel use of existing information to maximize the likelihood of obtaining an adequate sample.

This section of the report describes the conceptual framework for the sample design, alternative sample plans considered, the role of the advisory group and the contractor consortium, the final sample design, specifications of the advisory group for questionnaire design, the field data collection, and response rates and weight adjustments.

Conceptual Framework

The Government recommended an initial framework for the sample design to the advisory group. The framework arose out of an interest in determining the type of information that would be most useful for the Congress, out of prior experience with the surveys of language minorities performed by the National Center for Education Statistics, and out of limitations on the study imposed by the mix of available information on which to base a sample design and the funds available to support the work.

The first constraint was to use a household rather than a school-based sample. A public school-based sample would not access private school enrollments or children who may have dropped out or who were never enrolled, a relatively sizable group among some of the language minorities, according to NCES analyses of the SIE. A household sample would not have this difficulty. Households would be selected for participation based on whether or not they used a language other than English either usually or often. NCES had used household language to define language minority persons under age 14 in the CPS and SIE, and the Government's preference was to have consistent definitions used in the CESS for the 5-14 year old group. Use of consistent definition of language minority groups in SIE and CESS would make the two surveys comparable. Further, if the SIE language use and proficiency questions were also asked in the CESS, the identification of a Measure of English Language Proficiency (MELP), as discussed in Chapter I, could be explored. Basically, combinations of "census-type" MELP questions would be used to predict limited English proficiency in the CESS. The MELP would later be applied to the larger sample in the SIE to obtain state level estimates of limited English proficient children.

The second constraint was to use a probability sample of all language minorities in the United States based on available information. The sample should represent all languages and tap areas of high concentration and low concentration of language minorities as well. The available information on which to base a sample of this type was limited: The 1970

Census mother tongue question, 1970 Census adjustments for more recent counts of births and deaths, Census updates for new houses, and a 1972 compliance survey of schools performed by the Office of Civil Rights (OCR) in DHEW. The OCR survey had requested school level information on numbers of children who were dominant in a language other than English.

The third constraint dealt with stratification of the sample. The Government wished for the sample to represent the total United States including Alaska and Hawaii, and for all languages and ages between 5-14 years combined. However, the sample should also represent two language groups (Spanish, all others), and four age groups (5-6, 7-8, 9-11, 12-14 years) within each of four subpopulation areas (California, Texas, New York, and the balance of the country).

Alternative Sample Plans

The CESS was originally designed to use a sample drawn from the Survey of Income and Education (SIE). The household language questions were to be used to select language minorities from the sample of 150,000 households. The plan was to follow up a probability sample of the language minority households to obtain data required for the CESS: the test of language proficiency. This plan had the advantage of simplicity and low cost. The language minority households already had been identified and no costs of household screening would be required. Further, the household language questions and other demographic information already had been obtained. However, the plan was dropped because the Bureau of the Census was not then equipped to perform the entire followup, including securing household cooperation and testing children in the age range required.

The second alternative sample plan was to use a general purpose sample drawn to be broadly representative of the population in the United States. A general purpose sample could be stratified for the purposes of the CESS on language (Spanish, all others) within subpopulation (four geographic areas). Households would be screened in the preselected population segments for language use and presence of children in the target age range. Given the cooperation of the household respondent, tests would be administered in the home. This strategy had the advantage of using preselected population areas where experienced interviewers and testers were known and available as a means to limit selection and training costs. However, the plan was not accepted because a standing sample may not represent known areas of language minority concentration and therefore suffer from inherent lack of face validity.

Role of the Advisory Group and the Contractor

The advisory group reviewed the prior survey work performed by NCES and agreed to the Government's constraints, which were to: (1) perform the study on a household sample rather than a school-based sample; (2) construct a national probability sample of all language minorities using information then available in the design; and (3) report estimates for two language groups (Spanish, all others) and four age groups (5-6, 7-8,

9-11, 12-14 years) within each of four subpopulations (California, Texas, New York, and the balance of the country). Individual members of the advisory group strongly urged upon the Government and its contractors selection of a special sample of Asian American language minorities. However, the screening costs to locate a second special language group, particularly a language group represented in low numbers in the population, were prohibitive and neither the Government nor its advisors were able to develop sources for the required funds.

Recommendations received from individual members of the advisory group nevertheless were instrumental in the final sample design along with concerns raised by language minorities within the consortium of contractors. Reviews of a proposed general purpose sample by selected advisory group members and by consultants to the contractor's consortium led to the development of a consortium proposal for a special purpose sample that eventually was used, as described below.

Final Sample Section

The CESS sample was designed to produce a 15% error variance on the national estimate of limited English proficient children. Estimates of limited English proficient children were to be provided as well for two language groups (Spanish, all others) and four age groups (5-6, 7-8, 9-11, 12-14 years) within each of four subpopulations (California, Texas, New York, and the remainder). A special purpose sample was designed to assure representation in areas where language minorities were located. The CESS sample covered 50 states and the District of Columbia, except for remote counties in Alaska. The sample was selected proportionate to separate measures of size of the Spanish and non-Spanish language minority population in primary sampling units (counties and large cities) and population segments. The measure of size was composed from information on the 1970 Census and 1972 Office for Civil Rights (OCR) data on school enrollments, and was adjusted to over-represent areas with higher concentrations of language minorities. The number of language minority households in each segment was estimated by combining the measure of size with information from the Survey of Income and Education (SIE).

Approximately 35,000 households were screened in the CESS to identify roughly 2,000 households where a language other than English was used usually or often and where children between the ages of 5-18 years were living. Only up to two children aged 5-14 years and one child 15-18 years were selected in each language minority household. The language test was administered only to the 5-14 year olds. The 15-18 year old sample was of interest for potential access to school records, which was of interest for the 5-14 year olds as well. Interviews were not obtained in households where occupants were not found at home after three repeated visits. There were also three repeated visits for the test administration, which was scheduled separately from the interviews. Details on the sample design and on weighting procedures are in Appendix B.

Questionnaire Design

Two questionnaires were designed relating to household characteristics. The first questionnaire in the CESS, the Household Screener (Appendix C), was used to select households in which a language other than English was used usually or often and in which children between the ages of 5 and 18 years were living. If a household met both conditions and the respondent agreed to participate, a series of additional questions was asked on the identity of all household members and each person's following characteristics: name, relationship to head of household, sex, date of birth, individual language usually spoken, other individual languages spoken often or at all, origin or descent, and country of birth. From the lists of names on this questionnaire, up to two children aged 5-14 years and one child aged 15-18 years were randomly selected. Each question was identical to questions asked in the SIE and used the same response options for language identification, origin or descent, and country of origin. On this section of the questionnaire, there were seven separate probes, all worded differently, to identify persons in the household who were not mentioned among the names first listed by the respondent.

The Household Questionnaire (Appendix D) was used to obtain additional information about cooperating households selected to participate. Items contained on the Household Questionnaire were drawn from the SIE as were items on the Screener but contained additional questions recommended by the advisory group. Information requested included household income and, for selected children, school attended or reason for not being in school, highest grade completed, school exposure for language training, school attended outside the U.S., language of instruction, respondent rating on child's English and non-English language proficiency (speak, understand, read and write separately), and language usually spoken to siblings and to best friends.

Both the Household Screener and Household Questionnaire were translated into Spanish.

Data Collection

Responsibility for data collection was divided between two members of the contractor's consortium. One subcontractor, located in Texas, assumed responsibility for data collection in California and Texas, while another subcontractor, located in Maryland, assumed responsibility for New York and the balance of the country.

The two subcontractors coordinated their training for interviewers under the management of the prime contractor. Training procedures included home study, large and small group sessions, demonstrations, exercises, and role playing. The prime contractor performed training for the test examiners. Examiners were provided complete test administration packages for training that included a videotaped demonstration and supervised exercises in test administration. There were 16 regional supervisors, 196 interviewers, 10 trouble shooters and 73 test administrators.

One of the criteria of selection of interviewers, in addition to pertinent experience and responsiveness of training, was familiarity with a language other than English. The language used in selection depended on the language expected to be found in households the interviewer would contact, and varied depending on the region of the country. Information on the language proficiency of interviewers is included in Appendix E. Small cards were printed in six languages (Chinese, French, Italian, Japanese, Polish, and Yiddish) other than Spanish informing the respondent that the interviewer would return with an interpreter if needed. Test examiners were not selected specifically for familiarity with a language other than English because the text was designed to assess English language proficiency only and was designed to replicate a school situation where the child would be administered a test in English. However, examiners had to be trained in special procedures for establishing rapport with children whose proficiency in English might be limited.

Quality control was maintained by intermittent visits during household interviewing and testing by the 10 trouble shooters and by the prime contractor's staff. The prime contractor's staff visited 12 of the field supervisors on site and observed selected test administrators. Interviewers were responsible for 100% field editing. Regional supervisors performed an edit on 100% of the interviews during the first week for each interviewer and performed a scan edit thereafter. Call-backs were made when necessary to obtain missing information. Ten percent of all completed interviews were verified by telephone calls to the respondent by the regional supervisor. One hundred percent of the questionnaires were further edited upon receipt in the contractor's central office. The tests were edited once by the regional supervisor and again by the subcontractor for data analysis, where they were computer scored.

All questionnaire data were entered directly from the form on which they were recorded to computer on a TI 770 interactive terminal with a 10% verification. Programmable data entry formats on the TI 770 enabled close monitoring of the input to assure conformity with the instrument being entered. All data used in estimating numbers of language minority and limited English proficient children received 100% verification.

Response Rates and Weight Adjustments

Response rates are provided in Table III-I for each of the four major subpopulations (California, Texas, New York, and the balance) separately for the Household Screener, Household Questionnaire, and the language instrument. Response rates are derived from the formula:

$$\text{Response Rate} = \frac{\textbf{Total Number Completed}}{\textbf{Total Number Eligible}} \times 100$$

Table III-1

Response Rates by Subpopulation for Household Screener and Questionnaire and for the Language Measurement and Assessment Inventory (LM&AI)

Component	California	Texas	New York	Remainder of U.S.	Total
Household Screener	82.3%	78.1%	72.6%	75.7%	76.2%
Household Question-naire	94.9%	90.4%	93.6%	94.6%	93.8%
LM&AI	74.0%	86.5%	86.1%	87.6%	84.6%

Household Screeners were counted complete only if all information necessary to complete the classification of the household as eligible was furnished directly by the respondent in the interview. This information included the household language questions and questions pertaining to presence of children aged 5-18 years. Households that upon inspection were either vacant or not a dwelling unit were not counted among the eligibles. Household, Questionnaires were considered complete if the respondent provided full information as requested *and* if the Household Screener was complete. The LM&AI was considered complete if the test was administered through to the last item, or if the test was discontinued because the child failed to answer a successive series of items, as specified in the test administration manual.

The total response rate for the Household Screener was 76.2%. Analysis of the reasons for the nonresponse revealed that 57 out of 7,925 nonresponding households were suspected to be language minority households based on neighbor information. The remaining nonresponding households were ineligible either because they were known not to be a language minority household from questionnaire responses (n=2,078) or were suspected not to be a language minority household from interviewer judgment or neighbor information (n=5,790). The total response rate for the Household Questionnaire was 93.8% nation-ally. Response rates for the subpopulations did not drop below 90.4%, suggesting that once a language minority household was located, cooperation was extremely high. The response rate for the language test nationally was 84.6%. The largest categories for nonresponse on the language test nationally (348 out of 2,257) were refusals by parents (n=127), and not available to test (n=120). Other reasons included breakoffs during testing (n=4), and wrong age form administered or unknown (n=97). The response rate on the language test was lowest in California, where generally more children were not available during the test period and more tests were not given for unspecified reasons.

Weight adjustments were performed for the probability of selection of each segment and for subsampling households within enumeration districts and children within households. Nonresponse adjustments were performed for the Household Screener, the Household Questionnaire, and the Language Measurement and Assessment Inventory. Adjustments were also made to the language minority estimates obtained on the SIE. Further information on weight adjustments is contained in Appendix C.

Sources of Error

Two types of errors may be present in estimates presented in this report: nonsampling and sampling errors. **Nonsampling errors** can be attributed to many sources, e.g., inability to obtain information about all cases in the sample, definitional difficulties, differences in the interpretation of questions, inability or unwillingness to provide correct information on the part of respondents, mistakes in recording or coding the data obtained, and other errors of collection, response, processing, coverage, and estimation of missing data. Nonsampling errors are those that also occur in complete censuses.

Sampling errors occur because observations were made only on a sample, not on the entire population of language minorities in the U.S. The particular sample used in this survey is only one of all the possible samples of the same size that could have been selected from the population of language minorities using the same sample design. Because each of the possible samples is unique, estimates derived from the different samples would differ from each other. The **standard error** of a survey estimate is a measure of the variation among all possible samples, and thus provides a measure of the precision with which an estimate from a particular sample approximates the population value.

As calculated for this report, the standard error also partially measures the effect of certain nonsampling errors but does not measure any systematic biases in the data. **Bias** is the difference, averaged over all possible samples, between the estimate and the population value. The accuracy of a survey result depends on both the standard error and the bias and other types of nonsampling error not measured by the standard error.

Interpretation of Errors

The sample estimate and an estimate of its standard error permit interval estimates to be constructed with prescribed confidence that the interval includes the population value. For a particular sample, therefore, one can say with specified confidence that the average of all possible samples (i.e., the population value) is included in the constructed interval. For this report confidence intervals were computed at a 95% level of confidence. This means that if many samples similar to that of the CESS were drawn, then estimates obtained from 95% of these samples would be expected to fall within the confidence interval defined by the CESS sample estimates; 2.5% would fall either below or above the interval.

IV. RESULTS OF THE HOUSEHOLD SURVEY TO ESTIMATE NUMBERS OF LIMITED ENGLISH PROFICIENT CHILDREN

Results of the Children's English and Services Study (CESS) are reported in three broad categories. The first category includes estimates of limited English proficient children. The second contains information on concentration of language minorities associated with limited English proficiency. The final category of results contains information on the relationship between limited English proficiency and other characteristics of children or households.

Estimates of Limited English Proficient Children

Results of the CESS are reported for two language groups (Spanish, and other), four ages (5-6, 7-8, 9-11, 12-14), four subpopulations (California, Texas, New York, and the balance of the country), and for each subpopulation by language group. Estimates provided for each of these categories included the number of language minorities, the number of limited English proficient (LEP) children, and the percent of LEP children among language minorities. Language minority was defined as persons living in households where a language other than English was used usually or often. LEP children were identified by their performance on the Language Measurement and Assessment Inventory. Confidence intervals are provided for the percent LEP. These results are shown in Table IV-1, Estimated English Proficient Children among Language Minorities by Subpopulation, Age, and Language Background.

The total number of language minority children aged 5-14 years in the U.S. in the Spring of 1978 was 3.8 million. Of these children, an estimated 2.4 million or 63.2% were limited in English proficiency (LEP). The confidence interval for the percent LEP was 55.5 and 70.9. That is, the true estimate of the percent LEP would be expected to fall within this range with 95% confidence. Other figures in Table IV-1 can be interpreted in a similar manner. No error variances are presented for the estimated number of language minorities of LEP children for reasons discussed elsewhere in this report (Appendix C), although these numbers should be understood as estimates rather than absolute values.

At least four aspects of the figures in Table IV-1 should be emphasized. First, an estimated 1.5 million or 62% of all LEP children live in three states–California, Texas, and New York. The percent of LEP children residing in California and Texas is nearly identical. The percent LEP children in New York is slightly higher than in these two states, and the percent of the remainder of the U.S. is somewhat lower.

Second, the percent LEP children by age does not vary greatly. The percent LEP children among all language groups at the higher ages is nearly as high as the percent at the lower ages, although the percent drops off slightly as age increases. A marked decrease in limited English oral proficiency might have been expected for older children, who may have had more exposure than younger children to English in school or other settings and thereby acquired some command of the language. Two factors may account for not finding such a decrease. One is that the test criterion for LEP includes reading and writing skills as well as skills in speaking and understanding. A second and related factor is that the objectives of the test, in the judgment of the advisory group, are graduated in difficulty to reflect skills typically expected in schools for children at each age from 5-14 years.

Table IV-1

Estimated Limited English Proficient Children
Among Language Minorities by Subpopulation, Age, and Language Background
(numbers reported in 000)

Category	Language Minorities[a]	Limited English Proficient[a]	Percent[b]	Confidence Interval[c]
Whole U.S.	3,812	2,409	63.2	55.5-70.9
Subpopulation				
California	855	594	69.5	57.9-81.1
Texas	630	438	69.6	57.8-81.4
New York	608	468	76.9	60.5-93.8
Remainder	1,718	908	52.9	40.8-65.0
Age				
5-6 years	722	484	67.0	57.9-76.1
7-8 years	780	534	68.4	56.6-80.2
9-11 years	1,099	652	59.3	46.7-71.9
12-14 years	1,210	740	61.1	52.9-69.3
Language Background				
Spanish				
California	654	502	76.7	71.4-82.0
Texas	602	438	72.8	65.3-80.2
New York	364	316	86.9	78.8-94.9
Remainder	770	488	63.4	49.3-77.5
Total	2,390	1,744	73.0	67.5-78.4
Other Non-English				
California	201	93	46.0	12.1-79.9
New York	245	152	62.0	32.2-91.9
Remainder[d]	977	421	43.1	30.3-56.0
Total	1,422	665	46.8	35.3-58.2

a. Figures may not total due to rounding.
b. Percents = 100 x (limited English proficient/language minorities).
c. There is a 95% confidence that the interval includes the value of the percent being estimated.
d. Texas included with the Remainder of the U.S.

Third, there are more Spanish language minorities nationally than all other minority languages combined. Further, Spanish LEP children represent a larger percent of Spanish language minorities than their LEP counterparts among other non-English languages. Spanish LEP children are found in greater proportions within each subpopulation than other non-English language children, and the percent Spanish LEP in the three major states--California, Texas, and New York--was greater than the percent LEP in the remainder of the country. The percent Spanish LEP in New York is particularly high.

Finally, the precent of non-Spanish, non-English children who are LEP in New York is greater by far than in other areas. However, estimates of non-Spanish, non-English LEP children should be interpreted with caution because of the size of the confidence intervals. The samples for Texas and the remainder of the country were combined in the non-Spanish, non-English analysis. The Texas sample was too small for an independent estimate.

Population Density

Density of the language minority population may increase opportunities to use and sustain familiarity with the non-English language and reduce opportunities to gain familiarity with English. Relatively more limited English proficient children would be expected where the density of language minorities is greatest.

An index of density of language minority persons was available from the adjusted size measure used to stratify the sample (see Chapter III). This measure expressed the percentage of the total population that was language minority in each segment. The results are shown in Table IV-2, Density by Subpopulation for Limited English Proficient (LEP) and Non-Limited English Proficient (NLEP) Children. A greater tendency was found for LEP as contrasted with NLEP children to be located in segments with greater density of language minorities in Texas, New York, and the remainder of the country. However, in California, LEP and NLEP children tended to be located in both dense and non-dense areas in roughly equal proportions. The tendency for LEP children to be found in areas that are densely populated with language minorities was most striking in New York.

The tendency to find LEP children in segments that are more densely concentrated with language minorities suggests that attempts to establish bilingual education would find eligible children in adequate numbers. However, the type of educational program that would be appropriate for these limited English proficient children could only be determined from far more detailed data on individual languages and from county level information. Further, concentration of LEP children may be an incomplete criterion for determining the appropriateness of a program in the absence of information on local conditions and parental preference.

Characteristics of Children and Households

Children with limited proficiency in English can be expected to possess a series of unique characteristics that differentiate them from children whose proficiency in English is not limited. The value of a series of such characteristics for differentiating limited English proficient children from the more proficient children was explored in the CESS. The purpose of this exploration was to provide preliminary information for deriving "census-type" questions to predict LEP. The characteristics included the following: ratings of

Table IV-2

Density by Supopulation for Limited English
Proficient (LEP) and Non-Limited English Proficient (NLEP) Children
(numbers reported in 000)[a]

Subpopulation	Type of Child		Total	Density Codes[b]			
				1-2	3-4	5-6	7-8
California	LEP	n	594	83	167	115	229
		%	70%	73%	53%	71%	86%
	NLEP	n	261	30	147	46	37
		%	30%	27%	47%	29%	14%
	Total	n	855	113	313	161	267
Texas	LEP	n	438	60	42	124	212
		%	70%	50%	77%	70%	76%
	NLEP	n	191	61	12	52	66
		%	30%	50%	23%	30%	24%
	Total	n	630	120	54	176	279
New York	LEP	n	468	11	247	75	135
		%	77%	28%	73%	83%	95%
	NLEP	n	141	28	90	15	7
		%	23%	72%	27%	17%	5%
	Total	n	608	39	337	90	143
Remainder	LEP	n	908	174	296	325	114
		%	53%	28%	58%	74%	70%
	NLEP	n	810	437	212	111	50
		%	47%	72%	42%	26%	30%
	Total	n	1,718	611	508	436	164

a. Number may not total due to rounding.
b. Percent language minority by density codes are Code 1-2 = 0-9%; 3-4 = 10-29%;
    5-6 = 30-49%; 7-8 = 50%+.

English proficiency by a household respondent, ratings of non-English proficiency, usual individual language, language used with siblings or friends, and country of origin. Additionally, household income was expected to differentiate limited English proficient children from those with greater proficiency in English.

Household respondents in the CESS were requested to rate the language proficiency of selected children in English and in the child's non-English language. The household respondent, for each language, was asked to indicate how well the child could speak, understand, read, or write the language. The categories of response were "very well," "well (all right)," "not so well," and "not at all." Children rated "not so well" or "not at all" in their English language ability would be expected to occur with greater frequency among children whose test scores indicate they are LEP. Similarly, children rated "well" or "very well" by household respondents in their English language ability would be expected to occur more frequently among children whose test scores indicate they are NLEP.

24

The results for 5-14 year old children nationally are shown in Table IV-3, English Language Ratings by Household Respondent of Limited English Proficient (LEP) and Non–Limited English Proficient (NLEP) Children. Inspection of Table IV-3 reveals that of the total number of children rated able to speak English "not so well" or "not at all," 93% were LEP and 7% were NLEP. For children rated "very well" or "well" on English proficiency, 59% were LEP and 41% were NLEP. An almost identical pattern was found for ratings of the child's ability to understand English. Based on these results, LEP could be predicted with 93% accuracy for children in the "not so well" or "not at all" categories. Conversely, prediction would be highly inaccurate with children in the "well" or "very well" categories. Ratings of ability to read and write in English also shown in Table IV-3 do not clearly differentiate LEP and NLEP children. The percentages of LEP and NLEP children at the two levels of rated proficiency differ little from the total percent LEP in the language minority population.

Differences between the ratings and the test information were evident. Although ratings of "not so well" and "not at all" for ability to speak and understand English showed promise as a predictor of LEP, these categories did not nearly represent the total number of children. Clearly, using household respondent ratings as a simple substitute for instructionally related test information is likely to lead to errors in classification of language minority children as LEP.

A more thorough examination of the potential of respondent ratings to predict LEP seems warranted. One suggested approach is to use combinations of "census-type" questions to predict LEP, as was explored in previous work by NCES prior to the CESS. Another approach would be to identify combinations of test items which constitute a student's total score, on the expectation that LEP can be predicted more accurately if the criterion is differentiated in terms of gradations of LEP or in terms of subskill areas such as oral proficiency and reading. In lieu of the additional analyses required to explore these alternatives, however, the most accurate estimate of LEP children based on a "census–type" question seems to be obtained on the question about speaking proficiency from the combined percentage of children rated "well," "not well," or "not at all." In the total population, this percentage was 64%, a close approximation of the total percent LEP shown in Table IV-1, which was 63.2%. It is possible that anything other than a "very well" response to the household question on speaking ability is a suggestion that the child may be experiencing difficulty in school.

Table IV-3

English Language Ratings by Household Respondent
of Limited English Proficient (LEP) and Non-Limited Proficient (NLEP) Children
(numbers reported in 000) [a,b]

Question	Type of Child		Total	Very Well or Well	Not Well or Not at All
How well does	LEP	n	2,381	1,928	453
(name of child)		%	64%	59%	93%
speak English?	NLEP	n	1,365	1,331	34
		%	36%	41%	7%
	Total	n	3,746	3,260	487
How well does	LEP	n	2,382	2,030	352
(name of child)		%	64%	60%	92%
understand	NLEP	n	1,358	1,326	32
spoken English?		%	36%	40%	8%
	Total	n	3,740	3,356	384
How well does	LEP	n	2,393	1,644	749
(name of child)		%	60%	61%	57%
read and write	NLEP	n	1,626	1,064	562
in English?		%	40%	39%	43%
	Total	n	4,019	2,708	1,311

a. Totals may not add due to rounding.

b. Totals may not correspond to totals in Table IV-1 because no adjustments for item non-response were performed. The range of item nonresponse on 1909 cases was 1.6% to 1.8% for the three questions. Also, errors in coding or interviewer procedure on a preliminary screening item may have led to an overestimate for the category "Not Well" or "Not at All." The error rates were as follows: Speak English .58%; Understand English .16%; Read and Write English 1.05%.

Information was also available on the relationship between tested proficiency in English and household respondent ratings of proficiency in a child's non-English language. This information could add to the prediction of LEP from household respondent data. Two types of non-English language proficiency were rated in the CESS: speaking and understanding, and reading and writing. Response categories were "very well," "well," "not so well," and "not at all." Results of analyses of these data are shown in Table IV-4, Non-English Language Ratings by Household Respondent of Limited English Proficient (LEP) and Non-Limited English Proficient (NLEP) Children. For the question on the child's proficiency in speaking and understanding the non-English language, 72% of the children rated "very well" or "well" were LEP, and 28% of the children were NLEP. The LEP and NLEP children were nearly evenly split for children rated not well or not at all. For the question on reading and writing in the non-English language, the percentage LEP and NLEP did not differ greatly from an even split. Neither question on proficiency in the non-English language added appreciably to the prediction of LEP from household data.

A series of language use questions was asked of the household respondent in the CESS as an additional effort to identify household information that predicts limited English proficiency. Two questions asked about language use were as follows: "What language does (name of child) usually speak?"; and "What other language does (name of child) usually speak?" Two questions asked about the context for language use were: "What language does (name of child) usually speak to his/her brothers and sisters?" and "What language does (name of child) usually speak to his/her best friends?" The results of analyses for these questions are presented in Table IV-5, Language Use for Limited English Proficient (LEP) and Non-Limited English Proficient (NLEP) Children.

The question on the usual individual language of the child did not differentiate LEP and NLEP children to a great degree. However, there was a tendency for LEP children to be found more frequently among those for whom a non-English response was given. NLEP children tended to occur more frequently among those for whom an English response was given. For the question about the second (other) individual language of the child, children for whom the respondent indicated English were 84% LEP and 16% NLEP. The most likely reason for finding a relationship between LEP and speaking English as the second individual language is that the response for the usual individual language may have been a non-English language. On the question about language spoken to siblings (brothers and sisters), children for whom a non-English response was given were 86% LEP and 14% NLEP. Finally, LEP and NLEP children were most clearly differentiated on the question about language spoken to best friends, where a non-English response classified 92% of the children as LEP.

Table IV-4

Non-English Language Ratings by Household Respondent of Limited English Proficient (LEP) and Non-Limited English Proficient (NLEP) Children (numbers reported in 000)[a,b]

Question	Type of Child		Total	Very Well or Well	Not Well or Not at All
How well does	LEP	n	2,381	1,680	701
(name of child)		%	64%	72%	49%
speak and understand	NLEP	n	1,366	639	727
(non-English language)?		%	36%	28%	51%
	Total	n	3,747	2,319	1,428
How well does (name	LEP	n	2,420	515	1,905
of child) read and		%	52%	41%	56%
write in (non-English	NLEP	n	2,220	733	1,486
language)?		%	48%	59%	44%
	Total	n	4,639	1,248	3,391

a. Totals may not add due to rounding.
b. Totals may not correspond to totals in Table IV-1 because no adjustments for item non-response were performed. The item nonresponse on 1909 cases was 1.52% and 1.94% for the two items shown. Also, errors in coding or interviewer procedure on a preliminary screening item may have led to an overestimate for the category "Not Well" or "Not at All." The error rates were as follows: Speak and Understand .37%; Read and Write 2.41%.

Table IV-5

Language Use for Limited English Proficient (LEP) and Non-Limited English Proficient (NLEP) Children (numbers reported in 000) [a,b]

Question	Type of Child		Total	English	Non-English
What language does	LEP	n	2,377	1,340	1,037
(name of child)		%	63%	56%	74%
usually speak?	NLEP	n	1,399	1,037	362
		%	37%	44%	26%
	Total	n	3,776	2,377	1,399
What other	LEP	n	1,835	872	963
language does		%	70%	84%	60%
(name of child)	NLEP	n	797	164	632
usually speak?		%	30%	16%	40%
	Total	n	2,632	1,036	1,596
What language does	LEP	n	2,224	1,414	810
(name of child)		%	64%	56%	86%
usually speak with	NLEP	n	1,245	1,115	130
his/her brothers		%	36%	44%	14%
and sisters?	Total	n	3,469	2,529	940
What language does	LEP	n	2,361	1,889	472
(name of child)		%	63%	59%	92%
usually speak with	NLEP	n	1,360	1,318	43
his/her best friend?		%	37%	41%	8%
	Total	n	3,721	3,216	515

a. Figures may not total due to rounding.
b. Totals may not correspond to totals in Table IV-I because no adjustments for item non-response were performed. The nonresponse levels for the items on 1909 cases was: usually speak .79%; other speak 21% (high mainly because in many cases no other language was spoken); brothers and sisters 8.12%; and best friends 2.62%.

29

Data were also available in the CESS of country of origin. Results of analyses of country of origin data are shown in Table IV-6, Country of Origin for Limited English Proficient (LEP) and Non-Limited English Proficient (NLEP) Children. Of the children not born in the U.S., 59% were LEP and 41% were NLEP. For children born in the U.S., 64% were LEP and 36% were NLEP. There appeared to be a modest tendency for language minority children born in the U.S. to be more LEP than their counterparts whose country of origin was outside the U.S. However, a sizable number of LEP children appeared among those born outside as well as inside the U.S.

The final piece of information to be reported for which a differentiation between LEP and NLEP children was attempted is household income. Results of analyses are presented in Table IV-7, Income Levels for Families with Limited English Proficient (LEP) and Non-- Limited English Proficient (NLEP) Children. Income levels were grouped to reveal most clearly overall trends in the results. Missing information due to refusals and a "don't know" response is grouped in Table IV-7 rather than shown as a nonresponse because the level of this missing information was high. For incomes above $15,000, 35% of the children are LEP and 65% are NLEP. Further, at the lower income levels, under $7,999, 77% of the children were LEP and 23% were NLEP. Household income appears to be a predictor of LEP, albeit an imperfect one.

Table IV-6

Country of Origin for Limited English Proficient (LEP)
and Non-Limited English Proficient (NLEP) Children
(number reported in 000)[a]

Type of Child		Total	Born in U.S.	Not Born in U.S.
LEP	n	2,362	1,763	599
	%	63%	64%	59%
NLEP	n	1,398	989	409
	%	37%	36%	41%
Total	n	3,760	2,751	1,008

a. Totals may not add due to rounding. Numbers may not correspond to numbers in Table IV-1 because no adjustments for item nonresponse were performed. The nonresponse on 1909 cases was 1.0%.

Table IV-7

Income Levels for Families with Limited English
Proficient (LEP) and Non-Limited English Proficient (NLEP) Children
(numbers reported in 000)[a]

Type of Child		Total	Missing[b]	$7,999	$8,000-$14,999	$15,000
LEP	n	2,409	737	746	628	298
	%	63%	68%	77%	69%	35%
NLEP	n	1,403	345	228	287	543
	%	37%	32%	23%	31%	65%
Total	n	3,812	1,082	974	916	840

a. Figures may not total due to rounding.
b. Missing data include refusals and don't know.

31

V. COMMENTS FROM ADVISORY GROUP

REVIEW OF REPORT
LANGUAGE MINORITY CHILDREN WITH LIMITED ENGLISH
PROFICIENCY IN THE UNITED STATES

Ernest J. Mazzone, Director
Bureau of Transitional Bilingual Education,
Massachusetts

The responsiveness of the National Institute of Education, the National Center for Education Statistics, and the United States Office of Education to the Congressional mandate to determine the proportion of language minority children with limited English proficiency has been in my view carefully thought out, clairvoyant in many ways and effectively executed.

No previous investigation of this type had been attempted before on the national level. This called for creative and bold decision-making, and the government accepted the challenge. Probably the most significant and creative aspect of the project was the methodology, for three very important content issues had to be resolved demanding a high level of coordination and acceptability to three principal constituencies: technical experts, Federal and State bilingual program staff, and language minority advocacy groups.

During my participation in this project, I always felt that there was *real* and *meaningful* participation from these three constituencies which formed the advisory body from the very beginning and I felt that it would lend some assurance that the direction and the purpose of the study would be on target and acceptable. This advisory group, in collaboration with the Government and the principal contractor, L. Miranda and Associates, Inc., of Washington, D.C., in an unprecedented way prepared the technical specifications of the study and monitored its execution through every significant phase.

Although one might say that the reviewers' insistence on including in the conceptual framework, *reading,* and *writing,* along with speaking and understanding in the definition of limited English-speaking ability anticipated by about one year changes to be made in the Bilingual Education Act, as amended in 1978, it was very clear to me and to many others that the four language skills had to be the sine qua non of any common-sense definition.

The decision by consent of all to go to the drawing boards to develop a set of instruments to meet the specifications of the study was courageous and innovative, for had it not been so, the study might have been a castastrophic failure. But the die was cast and a set of rigid and comprehensive specifications were drawn for this purpose. The implementation of those specifications was a model of responsiveness, hard work, and diligently executed activities, including several field tests and pilot tests nationwide.

A number of hurdles had to be overcome in developing the conceptual framework and survey procedures for estimating the number of limited English proficient children. Several alternatives were examined. Because of the constraints of time, money and lack of fully equipped resources in the Government, the consultants to the contractor with advisory group members settled on a special purpose sample which would be adequate to carry out the mandate. The details of activities and decisions on this issue are quite adequately and clearly covered in the report. I believe it is significant to note that the data collection progress was meticulous and conscientious and adhered to the specifications in such things as the training of the interviewers and the insistence that they be familiar with a language other than English and with the high response rate for the household screener, questionnaire and language test.

After reading pages IV-5 (23) through IV-7 (25) several times and at several different settings, I still find it hard to reconcile the statements on the bottom of pages IV-5 and top of IV-7 with the data on population density (page 23, fifth paragraph, second sentence). The statement: "However, the type. . .on local conditions and parental preference" ignores State and Federal policy which requires bilingual-bicultural instruction for LEPs. I feel that statement is inappropriate here.

I would add one or two words of caution to those attempting to use rating from the household survey as a basis of estimating LEPs. Although there may be a coincidence of concurrence between *actual test data results* and *ratings,* the inference that the latter is as reliable a predictor of LEP as the former has not been established. This is not to preclude that more research on the subject is not needed. It should also be remembered that the development of the LARMI happened precisely because the reviewer's group found that opinion ratings were an inadequate measure of LEP.

April 28, 1980

Dr. John Chambers
NIE Associate
National Institute of Education
Reading and Language Studies
STOP 6
1200 19th Street, N.W.
Washington, D.C.   20208

Dear Dr. Chambers:

Thank you for inviting my comments relative to the draft report, "Language Minority Children with Limited English Proficiency in the United States, Spring 1978." It was my privilege to serve as a member of the Advisory Group for the Children's English and Services Study (CESS); I was designated by the Chief State School Officer to represent bilingual education in the state of Indiana. Although no longer with the Indiana State Education Agency, I continue to work with a Title IV (Civil Rights Act) project which provides training and technical assistance to school districts in Texas and New Mexico in the areas of Title VI compliance and equal educational opportunity for children.

Specifically, you are requesting a review of the summarization report of the CESS to determine whether the report:

1. interprets my recommendations during the design phase of the study accurately;

2. carries out my recommendations relative to the language assessment instrument;

3. responds to Legislative mandates in the Educational Amendments of 1974; and

4. shows credible results based on my experience in the field.

Each of the above will be discussed in the corresponding order, although there may be some overlap among the different areas.

1. **Recommendations relative to the study design.**

It was readily apparent at the first meeting in Washington that the members of the advisory group/reviewers' team had been convened to validate (rubber stamp?) prior research efforts undertaken by the National Center for Education Statistics (NCES) – especially the Measure of English Language Proficiency (MELP) – regarding the number of limited English speaking ability (LESA) children in the United States. The group's consensus was that, while the NCES investigations greatly contributed to the data base necessary to determine the number of LESA children, a nationwide needs assessment had to be conducted in order to more accurately determine the number and the educational needs of these students.

Personally, I voiced two main concerns which I asked the group to consider in the design of the study:

a. that the MELP was not an adequate assessment of limited English proficiency. It was my contention that MELP questions such as, "How well does your child speak English?" would not provide objective/accurate data required for a national count. The results of the CESS proved this assumption to be correct. On the MELP's question regarding a child's proficiency in speaking English, approximately 60% of those children rated "very well" or "well" by their parents turned out to be of limited English proficiency (LEP).

b. that the Government was defining LESA too narrowly by including only speaking and listening skills in the study. It was the government's contention that "understanding" referred to "listening" in the Legislative definition of LESA. I urged a closer look at the language in Section 703 (a) (1) of the Act, whereby LESAs are defined as individuals who "have difficulty speaking and *understanding instruction* in the English language" (emphasis added). To me, *instruction* clearly implied the inclusion of listening, speaking, reading and writing skills in English.

After a lengthy discussion on the point, the group recommended that a test be developed to measure

age-specific speaking, listening, reading and writing
skills in English. The Government agreed to allow
the advisory group to set the test specifications,
determine the criterion score (cut-off for determining
LEP/non-LEP, now changed from LESA) and assist in
the development of the sample design. The advisory
group was also able to provide considerable input
regarding the field test procedures in the development
of the language assessment instrument. The recommendations of the group as a whole were closely adhered to by
the Government and the contractor, L. Miranda and Associates.

2. Recommendations relative to the Language Assessment Instrument.

I was a member of the subgroup that formulated the content
objectives for the Language Measurement and Assessment
Inventory (LM&AI). The objectives recommended were those
that children ages 5-14 would be expected to perform in order
to profit from instruction in an all-English language environment. Items assessing each content objective were field tested
on three successive versions of the LM&AI. Although I did not
see the final version of the instrument, the meetings held prior
to the field test left no doubt that the persons responsible for
the final test items were following the recommendations of
the advisory group. I personally provided the objectives for
reading; the test items for reading followed my recommended
specifications. It should also be pointed out that members of
the advisory group participated in field testing the design in
their respective states. Thus, the advisory group was not solely
advisory in nature, but rather participated in almost every facet
of the study.

3. The legislative mandates.

The Children's English and Services Study was designed and
conducted in two parts. My comments refer only to that part
of the study which deals with the assessment of English language
proficiency in minority children and the resulting estimated
number of children with limited English proficiency in the
United States. A second part of the study regarding the educational needs of the LEP children and the types of service being
provided these children by the schools was conducted as part of
the CESS. The questionnaire used in the services part of the
study is quite thorough; it too was designed for the most part by

members of the advisory group. When combined, the language and the service studies most assuredly meet the legislative mandates.

It was a great personal satisfaction to note that my recommendation to include reading and writing was in step with, or a step ahead of, the new legislation of 1978. The fact that the group acted on the recommendation prevented the study from becoming obsolete upon the enactment of the Educational Amendments of 1978. Thus, the study not only responds to the legislative mandates of 1974, but also to the new legislative definition of limited English proficiency of 1978.

4. Credibility of the results.

The results of the CESS are entirely credible based on my experiences in the field. In Texas, for example, the study shows for 1978 an estimated total of 438,000 children of limited English proficiency. An OCR compliance survey for 1976-1977 not only supports the figures but also justifies the advisory group's recommendations to conduct the CESS in such detail. The OCR study ("Directory of Elementary and Secondary School Districts, and Schools in Selected School Districts: School Year 1976-1977, Volume I") lists a nationwide number of *identified* LEP students in *selected* school districts of 1,038,248. *Selected* Texas schools identify 279,681 LEP students in the OCR report. The report of all the Texas schools would undoubtedly bring the OCR total closer to the CESS estimation of 438,000.

The OCR report also indicated that 41% of the identified LEP children are enrolled in bilingual education programs nationwide. In Texas, 40% of the students reported in the survey are enrolled in bilingual education programs.

The Mexican American Legal Defense and Educational Fund (MALDEF) has brought a motion to enforce the Fourteenth Amendment to the U.S. Constitution, Section 601 of the Civil Rights Act of 1964 (Title VI), 42 U.S.C. 2000d, and Section 204(f) of the Equal Educational Opportunity Act of 1974 (EEOA), codified at 20 U.S.C. § 1703(f), in the *U.S. v Texas* law suit (Civil Act. 5281). The Texas Education Agency is charged with a failure to provide bilingual education to LEP students in the state of Texas. A ruling on the case is expected shortly.[6] Currently there are 86 school districts in Texas that are implementing a Lau plan pursuant to an OCR finding of noncompliance in the area. It is my belief that were all those data to be collected by individual states, the number of LEP students estimated by the CESS would prove to be conservative.

Dr. John Chambers
NIE Reading and Language Studies
April 10, 1980
Page Five

I applaud the efforts of NIE, NCES, and L. Miranda and Associates in responding to the congressional mandates.

Once more, thank you for inviting me to review the study. It was indeed a pleasure to have participated in this endeavor.

Sincerely,

Elena Vergara
Director, IDRA Center for
  Equity in Education

RESPONSE

LANGUAGE MINORITY CHILDREN WITH LIMITED ENGLISH PROFICIENCY IN THE UNITED STATES

The Congressional intent under Title VII of the Bilingual Education Act to identify limited English speaking children was one of the most complex tasks undertaken by the National Institute of Education (NIE) and National Center for Education Statistics (NCES). This program attempted to identify children who came from environments where a language other than English was dominant and whose native language was other than English or who were born outside the U.S. The project was carefully coordinated with a broad spectrum of State and Federal personnel. The hope of the committee was to accomplish something that all others had failed to do. The project was attempting to break new ground.

Although many professionals were involved in the early stages of the development, apparently the limitations of funds did not allow us to follow through to the end of the survey to review, comment, or participate in the deliberations which ultimately revised some of the survey's parameters, nor were we able to review the results before the initial release of the findings. The delays encountered in initiating the survey, the difficulties in finding students and gaining access to schools and their records, the necessity to re-enter districts to find more students, etc., raise serious questions whether the survey is as statistically sound as its original design, and whether this report can be used as a basis for policy making by the Congress. Unfortunately, none of these problems was identified in the body of the report, nor were the necessary adjustments noted.

I'm sympathetic to the writer's dilemma——that of describing the results of the survey in layman's language, and at the same time providing sufficient statistics and narrative to gain the confidence of the reader that the survey was properly administered and did what it purported to do. Unfortunately, there is an almost total absence of statistical data which did not enable me to adequately evaluate the report's conclusions. In spite of these data limitations, I've identified two of the most obvious flaws which limit the usefulness of this report. They are as follows:

1. Although not a statistical matter, I find the use of the phrase "able to profit from instruction in English" totally misleading. It implies that children who score below the cutting score will not benefit from instruction in English. This concept and the definition of the cutting score is completely foreign to the deliberations of the committee. What was agreed to was that children scoring below the cutting score probably needed additional service so they could become fluent in English and have the opportunity to reach their full educational potential in English. In fact, one of the study's objectives was to identify those kinds of services which would benefit most those children who have limited English proficiency.

2. The number of children classified as Limited English Proficiency (LEP) was considerably higher than expected. This is particularly true when compared to the count made in California during the same school year but prior to the initial survey. Although they were constructed differently they should have realized comparable results. The CESS used a small statistical sample whereas California conducted their survey over the entire student population. One would expect differences; however, not twice as many. It appears obvious that the CESS estimates are somehow skewed and I submit two of the most obvious reasons:

    a. Because of dollar considerations, survey population samples were drawn from high population areas (urban) and in areas where there were a high concentration of non-English speaking homes (often low income). As indicated in Table IV-2 and IV-7, there was a significant increase in the number of LEP children in high density (urban, Table IV-2) and low income areas (Table IV-7). It would appear that samples were inadvertently skewed and the findings were not adjusted to compensate for the factor. We were told that in California and Texas the survey was not well received in the field. In order to gain a large enough sample size in California the survey teams had to return later and conduct a second survey in the Fall. I understand that these additional samples were taken largely from urban and/or low income areas, adding to potential data distortion from the design. I also understand that only eight percent of the total original sample design was gathered in Texas—a size which raises a serious question concerning statistical validity.

    b. The ability of the test (LM&AI) to correctly classify the child as LEP or NLEP is also questioned. I would suggest that using preselected criterion groups of high or low scoring children produced an artificially high reliability. The report acknowledges this. However, under actual survey conditions which occurred for the broad spectrum of populace rather than a preselected group, the reliability would be considerably reduced and thus the confidence of the estimates must be reduced. Using the values of the standard error of measurement points this out.

When the reported 95% confidence interval was established around the cut off score for age 5 clients, it appears that approximately 31 (45%) of the 69 sample clients could have been misclassified in the actual survey rather than the four identified in the field test. I believe this is too wide a discrepancy to ignore. It suggests that the results were very unreliable.

Based on this preliminary and hurried review, I strongly recommend that the committee be reconvened to review and analyze the data and the circumstances encountered during the survey, and further recommend that the release of any findings be held until such time.

COLORADO DEPARTMENT OF EDUCATION

Reviewed by:

Robin Johnston
Assistant to the Commissioner

in collaboration with:

Dean C. Hirt, Executive Director
School Finance and Data Services

APPENDIX A

CHARACTERISTICS OF THE LANGUAGE
MEASUREMENT AND ASSESSMENT INVENTORY

The Language Measurement and Assessement Inventory (LM&AI) was designed to identify limited English proficient children in the Children's English and Services Study, a survey of language minorities in the United States. The survey provided estimates of the number of limited English proficient (LEP) children in the country living in households where a language other than English was spoken in the Spring of 1978. The test measured proficiency in speaking, understanding, reading and writing in English. It was designed to follow specifications of an advisory group composed of State representatives in bilingual education, assessment, and data collection.

The test was domain referenced for objectives in that, in the judgment of the advisory group, children at ages from 5-14 years would be expected to perform in order to profit from instruction in an all-English language educational environment. The LM&AI was developed in successive versions throughout three field tests. The final field test was performed on 789 children in three school districts in the Southwest, Southeast, and Northwest. Characteristics of this final version of the instrument are described in the following tables. The content of the test is shown in Table A-1, Domain-Referenced Content Objectives on the Language Measurement and Assessment Inventory.

Empirical data identifying language skills that are essential for limited English proficient children to function effectively in an all-English instructional medium were not available when the test was developed. Studies to identify such language skills are only beginning to be performed. In lieu of empirical data, informed judgment of an advisory group with substantial experience in education of limited English proficient children was considered crucial for identification of the objectives. Beyond professional judgment in formulating the objectives, however, items designed to assess the objectives at each age level were required by the advisory group to discriminate between students classified by schools as (1) limited in English proficiency or (2) fluent English speakers. Thus, the item selection was backed by empirical data showing that the items differentiated these two groups, and that fluent English speaking children tended to perform well on the items.

The number and type of items in two broad groupings, oral and written content, are show in Table A-2, Content Specifications by Age Level for the Language Measurement and Assessment Inventory. The total number of items per age form is shown at the bottom of the table.

**Domain-Referenced Content Objectives on
the Language Measurement and Assessment Inventory**

Skill Area	Mode	Subtest	Objective and Age Range
Speaking	Oral	Correct Usage	Given an incomplete sentence, the child will select the appropriate verb tense to complete the sentence. (Ages 5-8 pictorial; 5-14 non-pictorial)
		Similarities	Within 25 seconds, the child will describe the common attributes of two objects. (Ages 5-14)
		Differences	Within 25 seconds, the child will describe the attributes making two objects dissimilar. (Ages 5-14)
Listening	Oral	Comprehension	The child is able to remember sufficient details from an oral presentation to respond to specific questions. (Ages 5-14)
			After hearing a narrative account, the child is able to place general incidents in proper sequence. (Ages 5-14)
			The child demonstrates understanding of coherent passage of connected text by responding correctly to questions regarding *implied* meaning of the passage. (Ages 7-14)
			Given a series of directions, the child is able to select the appropriate product resulting from execution of the directions. (Ages 7-14)
	Written	Idiomatic Expressions	Given an idiomatic expression, the child will demonstrate an understanding of its meaning by selecting the appropriate response that best represents contextual use of the idiom. (Ages 7-14)

Skill Area	Mode	Subtest	Objective and Age Range
	Written	Cloze	The child will demonstrate understanding of commonly used words by selecting the appropriate word to complete a sentence. (Ages 8-14)
Reading	Oral	Word Recognition	The child will be able to recognize and pronounce correctly printed words, following 2-second exposure. (Ages 6-14)
	Written	Comprehension	Given a passage to read silently, the child is able to demonstrate understanding by selecting the main idea conveyed. (Ages 7-14)
			The child demonstrates understanding of a coherent passage of connected text by responding correctly to questions regarding the *literal* content of the passage. (Ages 7-14)
			The child demonstrates understanding of a coherent passage of connected text by responding correctly to questions regarding *implied* meaning of the passage. (Ages 7-14)
		Sequence	Given a passage to read silently, the child is able to recognize sequential relationships among two or more ideas. (Ages 8-14)
Writing	Written	Punctuation	The child is able to use punctuation conventions by selecting correctly punctuated phrases from among incorrect alternatives. (Ages 9-14)

Skill Area	Mode	Subtest	Objective and Age Range
		Capitalization	The child will demonstrate mastery of rules of capitalization by selecting correctly capitalized sentence segments from among incorrect alternatives. (Age 8-10)
		Synonyms	Given a stimulus word, the child will be able to select a synonym from a series of alternatives. (Ages 7-14)
		Antonyms	Given a stimulus word, the child will be able to select an antonym from a series of alternatives. (Ages 7-11, 13-14)

Table A-2

Content Specifications by Age Level for the Language Measurement and Assessment Inventory

Content Area	Number of Items by Age									
	5	6	7	8	9	10	11	12	13	14
Oral Tests										
Word Recognition	—	15	6	6	7	7	7	7	7	7
Oral Comprehension	4	4	2	2	3	7	4	4	4	4
Correct Usage: Pictorial	5	6	6	3	—	—	—	—	—	—
Correct Usage: Non-Pictorial	7	3	8	6	5	2	4	3	4	6
Similarities	3	3	3	2	2	2	2	2	2	2
Differences	3	3	3	2	2	2	2	2	2	2
Written Tests										
Written Comperhension	—	—	2	2	3	3	3	4	4	4
Cloze	—	—	3	3	3	3	3	7	7	7
Sequence	—									
Idiomatic Expressions	—	—	2	2	2	2	1	2	3	3
Synonyms	—	—	3	3	3	4	4	3	2	3
Antonyms	—	—	3	3	3	3	4	5	6	4
Capitalization	—	—	—	2	2	3	—	—	—	—
Punctuation	—	—	—	—	4	4	7	3	5	5
Total	22	34	41	36	43	47	46	48	52	53

Psychometric characteristics of the age forms are shown in Table A-3, Means, Standard Deviations, and Reliabilities (coefficient alpha) for the Language Measurement and Assessment Inventory. The number of students at each age who were designated by schools as fluent or limited in English proficiency in the third field test is shown, accompanied by means and standard deviations for each group. Reliabilities (coefficient alpha) are shown for the total group to whom the test was administered at each age level. Reliabilities reported are subject to influences from using extreme scoring groups, the limited English proficient children and fluent English speakers. The result of this influence generally will be to increase the reliabilities over what would be obtained with a more continuous distribution of scores.

The results of analyses to select a criterion score for classifying children as limited vs. proficient in English are shown in Table A-4, Classification Errors in Selection of a Criterion Score on the Language Measurement and Assessment Inventory. The column headed Proficiency in English on the Predictor is the classification of children as fluent or limited in English by the LM&AI. The column headed Proficiency in English on the Criterion is the school classification of children as limited or proficient in English. The cell entries are the number of children correctly and incorrectly classified in the third field test when the critical score indicated in the next column is used. Children whose scores fall below this point were designated limited in English proficiency, whereas children whose scores fall at or above this point were classified fluent in English. The next column shows the percent accuracy. Accurate classifications result when children are classified fluent on both the criterion and the predictor. The percent accuracy is the sum of limited and fluent accurate classifications divided by the total number of children at each age converted to a percent. It is of interest to note that the critical score shown in Table A-4 is approximately one standard deviation above the means shown in Table A-3 for the limited English proficient children, regardless of age.

Although the instrument appeared to have acceptable test characteristics for making estimates in a national sample, a number of cautions about the instrument are warranted. First, the instrument was designed in the context of a national survey specifically to differentiate children who would have difficulty profiting from instruction in English from those who would succeed. The instrument was *not* designed for placement or diagnosis with individual children in educational settings. The subtests in speaking, understanding, reading, and writing do not contain sufficient numbers of items to broadly represent the full domain of skills in each area. A second caution is that the instrument was designed in a specific fashion that resulted in an unknown level of cultural bias. That is, to the extent that placement decisions in the field test for children with limited skills in English were culturally biased, whether from test scores or teacher judgments, to the same extent the instrument is biased because it was designed to replicate those decisions. It was important for the instrument to have face validity and statistical validity for school practitioners irrespective of potential cultural biases inherent in their decision making processes. A third caution is that items on the test are not "pure" measures of English language proficiency. In some cases, the items assess English language proficiency, memory, and cognitive ability. The intermingling of these potentially disparate constructs was intentional to give the items as much validity for representing important school tasks as possible.

Table A-3

**Means, Standard Deviations, and Reliabilities (Coefficient Alpha)
for the Language Measurement and Assessment Inventory**

Age Form	Proficiency in English	Number of Students	Mean[a]	Standard Deviation	Reliability
5	Fluent	32	31.56	6.18	.91
	Limited	37	10.22	7.60	
6	Fluent	27	45.33	8.58	.91
	Limited	44	17.52	8.85	
7	Fluent	31	57.45	8.43	.92
	Limited	36	27.50	11.11	
8	Fluent	36	51.89	9.42	.87
	Limited	28	27.43	9.45	
9	Fluent	35	60.57	10.37	.90
	Limited	32	28.75	13.64	
10	Fluent	35	67.97	11.49	.88
	Limited	36	35.72	11.89	
11	Fluent	34	56.85	5.61	.88
	Limited	44	34.82	11.96	
12	Fluent	33	59.51	13.07	.86
	Limited	22	34.27	10.32	
13	Fluent	42	60.98	5.79	.91
	Limited	25	37.08	10.15	
14	Fluent	49	66.92	21.62	.86
	Limited	33	36.27	13.54	

a. Some of the items involved a production response. Therefore the means could be larger than the total number of items.

Table A-4

Classification Errors in Selection of a Criterion Score on the Language Measurement and Assessment Inventory

AGE	Proficiency in English on the Predictor	Proficiency in English on the Criterion[a] Fluent	Limited	Critical Score	Percent Accuracy[b]
5	Fluent	32	0	19	90.0
	Limited	7	30		
6	Fluent	27	0	26	87.3
	Limited	9	35		
7	Fluent	31	0	39	89.6
	Limited	7	29		
8	Fluent	36	0	39	95.3
	Limited	3	25		
9	Fluent	35	0	43	91.0
	Limited	6	26		
10	Fluent	35	0	49	91.5
	Limited	6	30		
11	Fluent	34	0	41	82.1
	Limited	14	30		
12	Fluent	27	6	47	83.6
	Limited	3	19		
13	Fluent	42	0	48	92.5
	Limited	5	20		
14	Fluent	39	10	52	82.9
	Limited	4	29		

a. Entries are number of cases in field test three.
b. For example, percent correct at age 5 equals 100 (32+30)/69=90.0.

Two comments about the procedure for selecting the criterion score are appropriate. First, the procedure is but one of a number of procedures that could have been used for this purpose. One alternative would be to select the criterion score based on a more continuous distribution of scores than tends to be obtained by using limited English proficient and fluent English speaking children. This alternative was not chosen by the advisory group because selection of the criterion score would have been ambiguous in the absence of two clearly defined groups. The advisory group generally felt that the procedure chosen provided the most useful information in the selection of items and the designation of a criterion score. The procedure was contrasted with a number of other approaches to determine which among them provided the lowest classification errors and the most direct interpretation. The other approaches included setting the cutting score at one standard deviation below the mean of the fluent English speaking group in the third field test, and using weighted combinations of subscores on the test to predict the criterion.

The discriminant function on the total score was the most satisfactory of the alternatives. A second comment about the procedures for selecting the criterion score is that the number of cases at each age in the third field test appears small relative to the number of cases on which tests are typically standardized. The purpose of the third field test, however, was not to produce standard scores or percentiles as with a standardized test but to select a criterion score and to inspect the classification errors for two totally different types of children. The magnitude of the classification errors in this instance is the condition for determining whether the procedure yields acceptable results.

APPENDIX B

SAMPLE DESIGN

A special purpose sample was used in the CESS to identify geographic areas where language minority populations were located. The sample was designed to produce a 15% error variance on the national estimate of limited English proficient children. Estimates of limited English proficient children were to be provided nationally and for two language groups (Spanish, other) and four age groups (5-6, 7-8, 9-11, 12-14 years) within each of four subpopulations (California, Texas, New York, and the remainder).

All of the approximately 3,000 counties and independent cities in the United States were stratified into the four geographic subpopulations: California, Texas, New York, and all others combined. Within each subpopulation, the counties and independent cities were stratified into eight categories by percent of the population with mother tongues other than English derived from updated tapes (Fourth and Fifth Count Tapes) on the 1970 Census. The percentages were determined separately for Spanish and all other non-English languages combined.

Two adjustments on the size of the population with mother tongues other than English were made prior to the calculation of percentages for the stratification. First, measures of size at the county level were adjusted for concentration of persons with non-English mother tongues on the assumption that limited English proficient children are more likely to be found in areas of high concentration. Second, the measures of the Spanish population at the county level were adjusted upward proportionate to the ratio nationally of (1) the mother tongue population reported in the 1970 Census to (2) estimates of the number of Spanish pupils reported in 1972 Office of Civil Rights (OCR) data on school enrollments in counties having 10,000 or more pupils.

Seventy-five counties and large cities across the country were then selected proportionate to their measures of size. That is, counties with a large measure of size were sampled at a higher rate. There were two exceptions. First, certain counties and large cities were selected in advance due to the large value of their adjusted size measure. Second, remote counties in Alaska were eliminated because of cost and interviewing difficulties in remote areas.

Within the 75 counties and large cities (primary sampling units) a total of 591 segments was selected. Each segment was composed of enumeration districts and block groups which were aggregated as necessary to produce a minimum of 30 year-round housing units. The segments were assigned to one of eight levels within each county or large city using percentages of children aged 5-14 with non-English mother tongues based on the adjusted size estimates. A higher probability of selection was given to high density segments, i.e., to segments with a higher proportion of households on the measure of size. The number of housing units chosen for sampling within each of the eight segment levels varied depending on the expected density of language minority households, i.e., of households where a language other than English was used usually or often. More households were selected in less dense segments because greater effort would be required when language minority households were scarce.

Number of language minority households by subpopulation (California, Texas, New York, and the balance) was estimated from the Survey of Income and Education (SIE). The expected number of language minority households within each level of segment size was estimated by converting in adjusted segment size measure (number of children) to a measure of households from knowledge on the SIE of the number of children per language minority household.

Results from the SIE were of further use in designing the sample. The SIE results indicated that there were roughly 2 million households with children in the 5-14 age range where a language other than English was spoken usually or often. Without stratification, one would expect about one household in 35 nationally to be a language minority household with children in the age range of interest. An unstratified sample would require screening 70,000 households with 100% response rate to obtain 2,000 language minority households. The stratified sample was designed to cut the number of screened households roughly in half. Thus, the approximate sample yield of language minority children could be estimated. What could not be determined was the number of these children who were limited in their proficiency in English. For planning purposes, a minimum estimate of one limited English proficient child for every five language minority children was used.

Screening of households in enumeration districts and block groups was performed using two criteria. Households were only selected if (1) a language other than English was used usually or often; and (2) children between the ages of 5 and 18 lived in the household. The 15-18 year old sample was of interest for school data, although the language test was administered only to the 5-14 year olds. Thus, all selected households were language minority with children in the age range of interest. The sampling plan within households was to select only up to two children 5-14 years of age and one child 15-18 years.

Six weight adjustments were used to obtain estimates in the CESS. A basic sampling weight was applied to each segment calculated from the probability of selection of the segment. The basic sampling weight was adjusted first based on the number of listed addresses compared to the actual number of dwelling units. The second weight adjustment was for subsampling children within dwelling units. Not all children within each dwelling unit had been selected, only up to two 5-14 year olds and one 15-18 year old. The next three adjustments were for nonresponse on the Household Screener, Household Questionnaire, and Language test. Finally, these weights were adjusted by age, sex, language, and subpopulation distribution to match the respective distribution of cases in the SIE. However, data from the SIE had been "aged" to account for births and deaths of children who moved into a new age category from 1976 to 1978. SIE estimates of language minority individuals would be expected to be more stable than those from the CESS due to the much larger sample.

A number of cautions are suggested about the sample design. First, data used in the sample design, although the most accurate then available, were nevertheless outdated. The sample, designed in early 1978, was based primarily on information from the 1970 Census, updated housing information, the 1972 OCR Compliance Survey, records of births and deaths, and the 1976 SIE. Since the design of the sample, the only improved information is from a more recent OCR survey. The information will not be improved substantially until the 1980 Census.

Second, the sample designing was complicated. Size estimates of individuals with mother tongues other than English were adjusted at the county level twice, once for concentration of non-English mother tongue persons from the 1970 Census and once for estimates of Spanish dominant children from the OCR survey. Further, the number of language minority households at the segment level was based on subpopulation level data from the SIE. These adjustments were desirable to improve the likelihood of locating 5-14 year old language minority children who were limited in English proficiency when only outdated information was available for the sample designed. The adjustments nevertheless appear complex because the sample could have been designed in a number of alternative ways.

Third, multiplying successive response weights may introduce progressive nonsampling error into the estimate. The nonresponse weights may be particularly influential in this effect. The response rate on the Household Screener nationally was just below 80%, whereas the response rate for the Household Questionnaire was over 90% and for the Language Measurement and Assessment Inventory it was 85%. One of the procedures used to verify the CESS estimate of language minorities, given the adjustments on the size estimate and the nonresponse adjustments, was to compare the CESS estimate with the estimate obtained in the SIE. The SIE was a much larger survey than the CESS, obtaining information from over 150,000 households in 1,000 primary sampling units compared with about 2,000 households in 75 primary sampling units in the CESS. The CESS weighted estimate of language minority children aged 5-14 years nationally was within 100 thousand of the weighted estimate on the SIE, 3.8 million, a reasonably close approximation that lent credibility to the complicated adjustments of the size measure and the successive non-response adjustments.

Fourth, error variances on the CESS for estimated numbers of language minorities and LEP children cannot be interpreted directly. Additional error was introduced to the CESS error variances from adjustments of the CESS age, sex, and language distributions to the SIE. Error variances on the SIE have not been calculated for the estimates of interest in the CESS. Further, SIE data to which the adjustments were made had been "aged" from 1976 to 1978 to reflect county reports of births and deaths by age, sex, and language. The extent to which reported births and deaths are inaccurate differentially for language minorities is unknown. Thus, a precise SIE adjustment would account for both the SIE error and the aging. However, error variances reported in the text, Table IV-1, for the estimated proportion of limited English proficient children among all language minorities are accurate because both the numerator and denominator of the proportion contained the SIE adjustment, and the two values cancel out.

Fifth, the sample did not include mobile homes or group housing units such as dormitories or flop houses. Although LEP children aged 5-14 years are unlikely to be found in group housing units, their prevalence in mobile homes is unknown.

Finally, Census reports of year-round housing units at the county level were applied to segment level data because neither time nor resources were available to update new housing development from county records. In only a single segment of 591 segments was the number of language minority children substantially different from the number expected. The weight was not trimmed for three reasons: (1) estimates of language minorities were to be adjusted to the age, sex, and language distribution in the SIE regardless, (2) estimates of LEP children would not be affected because the proportion LEP in the segment did not differ meaningfully from the proportion in the subpopulation; and (3) trimmed weights would produce unknown levels of bias and, given the negligible effect of the weight on the estimates of language minorities and LEP children, are less preferable than maintaining a bias-free estimate.

APPENDIX C

HOUSEHOLD SCREENER QUESTIONNAIRE

CHILDREN'S ENGLISH AND
SERVICES STUDY

HOUSEHOLD SCREENER

Collected for:
National Institute of Education,
National Center for Education Statistics
and
United States Office of Education

OMB NO: 51-S78001

Expires: December 1978

Collected by:
L. Miranda and Associates
with
Westat, Inc.
and
Resources Development Institute

OFFICE USE ONLY

Date Received: _____
ID Number: _____
Preliminary Status: _____
Final Status: _____

ASSIGNMENT BOX:

PSU: _____   SEG: _____   DU: _____

ADDRESS: _____
        (NUMBER)   (STREET)

_____
(APT. NO.)

_____
(CITY)   (STATE)

INTRODUCTION

Hello, I'm _____ from (RESEARCH COMPANY.) (SHOW ID BADGE.) We are conducting a study for the Education Division of the Department of Health, Education, and Welfare on the educational needs of children. The purpose of the study is to provide Congress and the President with information required to improve the education received by children who come from homes where languages other than English are spoken. (HAND LETTER, THEN SAY) Please read this. If you have any questions, I'll be happy to answer. (AFTER RESPONDENT HAS READ THE LETTER, SAY) Let me refer you back to the last two paragraphs. You understand that the information we collect from you will not be voluntarily disclosed for any purposes, and you are not required to take part in the interview and may refuse to answer any question you do not want to answer.

ASK AT SAMPLED HOUSEHOLD AND RECORD VERBATIM. IF A SINGLE YEAR OR RANGE IS GIVEN THAT DEFINITELY FITS ONE OF THE STATED CATEGORIES, CHECK APPROPRIATE CIRCLE: OTHERWISE CHECK D.K.

The sample of households we visit is scientifically selected to represent all households in our country. In order to be certain our sample is correct, I need to ask:

When was this structure originally built? _____
                                   Year / Range

◯ 1970 or later   ◯ Before 1970   ◯ D.K., No idea, etc.   ◯ Unoccupied, Vacant

ASSIGNED TO (PRINT): _____   _____
                      (INTERVIEWER NAME)   (INTERVIEWER NUMBER)

REASSIGNED TO (PRINT): _____   _____
                       (INTERVIEWER NAME)   (INTERVIEWER NUMBER)

_____   _____
(INTERVIEWER NAME)   (INTERVIEWER NUMBER)

INTERVIEW ONLY A PERSON IN THE HOUSEHOLD 16 YEARS OLD OR OLDER.

```
┌─────────────────────────────────┐
│ TIME                    AM      │
│ BEGAN _____  PM      │
└─────────────────────────────────┘
```

S-1.　　Are there any children living in your household who are between 5 and 18 years of age?

```
                                              Yes. . . . . . . . . . . . . 1
                                              No . . . . . . . . . . . . . 2
```

S-2.　　What language do the people in this household <u>usually</u> speak at home? (CIRCLE ONE CODE ONLY)

English. 01	Greek 07	Russian 14
Arabic 02	Italian 08	Scandinavian Language . 15
Chinese. 03	Japanese. 09	Spanish 16
Filipino 04	Korean. 10	Vietnamese. 17
(Tagalog, Ilocano)	Navajo. 11	Yiddish 18
French 05	Polish. 12	Other (SPECIFY) 19
German 06	Portugese 13	_____

S-3.　　Do the people in this household <u>often</u> speak any other language here at home?

```
                                              Yes . . . . . . . . . . . . 1  (BOX A)
                                              No  . . . . . . . . . . . . 2  (BOX C)
```

```
┌──────────────────────────────────────────────────────────────────────────────┐
│ BOX A   IF "YES" TO S-3, ASK:  What is that language?  (CIRCLE ONE CODE ONLY)   │
│                                                                                │
│ English. . . . . . . 01    Greek . . . . . . . . 07    Russian . . . . . . . 14 │
│ Arabic . . . . . . . 02    Italian . . . . . . . 08    Scandinavian Language 15 │
│ Chinese. . . . . . . 03    Japanese. . . . . . . 09    Spanish . . . . . . . 16 │
│ Filipino . . . . . . 04    Korean. . . . . . . . 10    Vietnamese. . . . . . 17 │
│    (Tagalog, Ilocano)      Navajo. . . . . . . . 11    Yiddish . . . . . . . 18 │
│ French . . . . . . . 05    Polish. . . . . . . . 12    Other (SPECIFY) . . . . 19 │
│ German . . . . . . . 06    Portugese . . . . . . 13    _____         │
│                                                                                │
│                          (BOX B)                                               │
└──────────────────────────────────────────────────────────────────────────────┘
```

```
┌──────────────────────────────────────────────────────────────────────────────┐
│ BOX B   (CIRCLE ONE):                                                           │
│                                                                                │
│          IF THERE ARE CHILDREN BETWEEN 5 AND 18 YEARS OF                        │
│          AGE LIVING IN HOUSEHOLD  (S-1, CODE 1) . . . . . . . . . 1  (S-6)      │
│                                                                                │
│          IF THERE ARE NO CHILDREN BETWEEN 5 AND 18 YEARS                        │
│          OF AGE LIVING IN HOUSEHOLD (S-1, CODE 2). . . . . . . . . 2  (S-24)    │
└──────────────────────────────────────────────────────────────────────────────┘
```

```
┌──────────────────────────────────────────────────────────────────────────────┐
│ BOX C   (CIRCLE ONE):                                                           │
│                                                                                │
│          IF ENGLISH IS <u>USUALLY</u> SPOKEN IN THE                             │
│          HOUSEHOLD (S-2, CODE 01) . . . . . . . . . . . . . . 1  (S-4)          │
│                                                                                │
│          IF ANOTHER LANGUAGE BESIDES ENGLISH IS USUALLY                         │
│          SPOKEN IN THE HOUSEHOLD (S-2, CODES 02-19) AND                         │
│          THERE ARE CHILDREN BETWEEN 5 AND 18 YEARS OF AGE                       │
│          LIVING IN THE HOUSEHOLD (S-1, CODE 1) . . . . . . . 2  (S-6)          │
│                                                                                │
│          IF ANOTHER LANGUAGE BESIDES ENGLISH IS USUALLY                         │
│          SPOKEN IN THE HOUSEHOLD (S-2, CODES 02-19) AND                         │
│          THERE ARE NO CHILDREN BETWEEN 5 AND 18 YEARS                           │
│          OF AGE LIVING IN THE HOUSEHOLD (S-1, CODE 2) . . . . 3  (S-24)         │
└──────────────────────────────────────────────────────────────────────────────┘
```

S-4.　　Is any <u>other</u> language spoken by the people who live in this household?

```
                                              Yes . . . . . . . . . . . . 1
                                              No  . . . . . . . . . . . . 2  (S-24)
```

S-5.　　What is that language? (CIRCLE ONE CODE ONLY)

English. 01	Greek 07	Russian 14
Arabic 02	Italian 08	Scandinavian Language . 15
Chinese. 03	Japanese. 09	Spanish 16
Filipino 04	Korean. 10	Vietnamese. 17
(Tagalog, Ilocano)	Navajo. 11	Yiddish 18
French 05	Polish. 12	Other (SPECIFY) 19
German 05	Portugese 13	_____

HOUSEHOLD ENUMERATION

S-6.   How many persons live in this household? _____
                                                    NUMBER

S-7.   What is the name of the head of this household? (ENTER NAME ON LINE 01 IN TABLE BELOW)

S-8.   And the other members of this household -- what are their names? Let's begin with everyone
       related to (HEAD). (BE SURE PERSON INCLUDES (HIMSELF/HERSELF)) (ENTER NAMES IN TABLE BELOW)

S-9.   Are there other persons living here who are not related to (HEAD)?
       (IF YES, ENTER NAMES IN TABLE BELOW)   Yes. . . 1   No. . . 2

S-10. I have listed (READ NAMES IN ORDER). Have I missed any babies or
       small children?   Yes. . . 1   No. . . 2

       Any lodgers, boarders, or persons in your employ who live here?   Yes. . . 1   No. . . 2

       Anyone who usually lives here but is away at present travelling,
       at school, or in a hospital?   Yes. . . 1   No. . . 2
       (IF YES, ENTER NAME IN TABLE BELOW)

S-7 - S-10 AFTER LISTING HOUSEHOLD, ASK S-11 THROUGH S-20 FOR EACH PERSON BEFORE ASKING FOR THE NEXT PERSON — ENTER LAST NAME OF HOUSEHOLD MEMBER ON FOLD-OUT PAGE.	S-11. What is (PERSON'S) relationship to (HEAD OF HOUSEHOLD)?	S-12. CODE SEX (ASK IF NOT OBVIOUS)	S-13. What is (HEAD/PERSON)'s date of birth? (OBTAIN AGE ON LAST BIRTHDAY IF DATE OF BIRTH IS UNKNOWN)	S-14. ENTER AGE USING DATE/AGE VERIFICATION CHART FOR CHILDREN BORN IN YEARS 1960 to 1973.	S-15. What language does (HEAD/PERSON) usually speak? (ENTER CODE FROM BELOW)	S-16. Does (HEAD/PERSON) speak any other language often? (IF NO, SKIP TO S-18)	S-17. What other language does (HEAD/PERSON) speak? (ENTER CODE FROM BELOW)	S-18. What is (HEAD/PERSON) origin or descent? (HAND CARD A ENTER UP TO THREE CODES FROM CODES PROVIDED BELOW)	S-19. Was (HEAD/PERSON) born in the United States? (IF YES, AND ANOTHER HH MEMBER, GO TO S-11 OTHERWISE GO TO S-21)	S-20. Where was (HEAD/PERSON) born? (ENTER CODE FROM BELOW)
Person Number First Name		M F	Mo / Da / Yr			Y N			Y N	
01	HEAD	1 2	/ /			1 2			1 2	
02		1 2	/ /			1 2			1 2	
03		1 2	/ /			1 2			1 2	
04		1 2	/ /			1 2			1 2	
05		1 2	/ /			1 2			1 2	
06		1 2	/ /			1 2			1 2	
07		1 2	/ /			1 2			1 2	
08		1 2	/ /			1 2			1 2	
09		1 2	/ /			1 2			1 2	
10		1 2	/ /			1 2			1 2	
11		1 2	/ /			1 2			1 2	
12		1 2	/ /			1 2			1 2	

ENTER THESE CODES IN APPROPRIATE COLUMN OF TABLE ABOVE

Language Spoken S-17		Origin/Descent S-18		Country of Birth S-20	
01 = English	11 = Navajo	01 = German	17 = Other Spanish	01 = Puerto Rican	18 = Scandinavia
02 = Arabic	12 = Polish	02 = Italian	18 = Portugese	02 = Other U.S. Terr.	19 = Vietnam
03 = Chinese	13 = Portugese	03 = Irish	19 = Am. Indian/Alaskan	03 = Canada	20 = Other (SPECIFY
04 = Filipino	14 = Russian	04 = French	Native	04 = China	COUNTRY IN
(Tagalog,	15 = Scandinavia	05 = Polish	20 = Negro	05 = Cuba	COLUMN BLOCK)
Ilocano)	16 = Spanish	06 = Russian	21 = Black	06 = England	
05 = French	17 = Vietnamese	07 = English	22 = Filipino	07 = France	
06 = German	18 = Yiddish	08 = Scottish	23 = Chinese	08 = Germany	
07 = Greek	19 = Other	09 = Welsh	24 = Japanese	09 = Greece	
08 = Italian	(SPECIFY	10 = Mexican Am.	25 = Korean	10 = Italy	
09 = Japanese	IN COLUMN	11 = Chicano	26 = Vietnamese	11 = Japan	
10 = Korean	BLOCK)	12 = Mexican	27 = Scandinavian	12 = Korea	
		13 = Mexicano	28 = Arabic	13 = Mexico	
		14 = Puerto Rican	29 = Greece	14 = Philippines	
		15 = Cuban	30 = Other (SPECIFY	15 = Poland	
		16 = Central or	IN COLUMN BLOCK)	16 = Portugal	
		South Am.	98 = Don't Know	17 = Russia	

S-21.   Is there anyone now away from home who usually lives here? (IF HOUSEHOLD MEMBER, ENTER NAME
        ON HOUSEHOLD ENUMERATION AND ASK S-11 THROUGH S-20)

                                                          Yes 1   No 2

S-22.   Do any of the persons in this household have a home anywhere else? (IF YES, PROBE FOR USUAL
        RESIDENCE. IF HOUSEHOLD MEMBER, ENTER NAME OF HOUSEHOLD ENUMERATION. IF NOT A HOUSEHOLD
        MEMBER, DRAW LINE THROUGH NAME ON HOUSEHOLD ENUMERATION.)

                                                          Yes 1   No 2

APPENDIX D

HOUSEHOLD QUESTIONNAIRE ITEMS

OMB No: 51-S78001
Approval Expires:
December, 1978

PSU / SEG / DU

CHILDREN'S ENGLISH & SERVICES STUDY

CONDUCTED FOR:

National Institute of Education,
National Center for Education Statistics,
and
The U.S. Office of Education

CONDUCTED BY:

L. Miranda & Associates, Inc.
with
Westat, Inc.
and
Resource Development Institute

HOUSEHOLD QUESTIONNAIRE

A.   YOU SHOULD NOW BE SPEAKING TO THE TARGET CHILD(REN)'S
     MOTHER, FATHER, OR GUARDIAN. AS A TRANSITION FROM THE
     SCREENER TO THE HOUSEHOLD QUESTIONNAIRE, READ THE
     FOLLOWING PARAGRAPH.

     As I told you, the purpose of this study is to provide
     Congress and the President with information required to
     improve the education received by children who come from
     homes where languages other than English are spoken. To
     provide this information, I would like to ask you some
     additional questions, ask *(TARGET CHILD(REN) 5-14)* some
     questions, and if your child(ren) is (are) enrolled in
     school, we would like your permission to get some
     information about what he (she) (they) is (are) being
     taught in school.

B.   VERIFY AGE AND NON-ENGLISH HOME LANGUAGE OF SELECTED CHILDREN.

C.   IF ERROR IN SCREENER-REPORTED AGE/NON-ENGLISH HOME LANGUAGE
     FOUND DURING INTERVIEW, EXPLAIN BELOW.

ENTER THE NAME(S) AND AGE(S) OF THE TARGET CHILD(REN) FROM THE HOUSEHOLD
ENUMERATION ON PAGE 3 OF THE SCREENER.

BOX A

ASK H-1 THROUGH H-32 FOR ONE TARGET CHILD BEFORE PROCEEDING WITH THE OTHER TARGET
CHILD(REN), IF ANY. IF THE TARGET CHILDREN HAVE DIFFERENT PARENTS OR GUARDIANS,
ASK ALL QUESTIONS APPROPRIATE FOR ONE PARENT BEFORE ASKING TO SPEAK TO THE SECOND
PARENT.

H-1.   Is *(TARGET CHILD)* enrolled or attending school now?

                         Yes ....

                         No ....

H-2.   Please tell me the name and address of the school *(TARGET CHILD)* is
         enrolled in. (CHILD MAY ATTEND TWO SCHOOLS. ALSO TRY TO OBTAIN THE
         NAME OF THE SCHOOL DISTRICT.)

H-3.   Is *(SCHOOL)* a public or private school?

                         <u>FIRST SCHOOL:</u>

                             Public ....

                             Private ....

                         <u>SECOND SCHOOL:</u>

                             Public ....

                             Private ....

BOX A	/////////	/////////	/////////

H-1.	......1*(H-2)* ......2*(H-5)*	......1*(H-2)* ......2*(H-5)*	......1*(H-2)* ......2*(H-5)*
H-2.	FIRST SCHOOL: Name:_____ Address:_____ _____ _____ Zip:_____ District:_____ SECOND SCHOOL: Name:_____ Address:_____ _____ _____ Zip:_____ District:_____	FIRST SCHOOL: Name:_____ Address:_____ _____ _____ Zip:_____ District:_____ SECOND SCHOOL: _____ _____ _____ _____ Zip:_____ District:_____	FIRST SCHOOL: Name:_____ Address:_____ _____ _____ Zip:_____ District:_____ SECOND SCHOOL: _____ _____ _____ _____ Zip:_____ District:_____
H-3.	...... 1 ...... 2 ...... 1 2	...... 1 ...... 2 ...... 1 2	...... 1 ...... 2 ...... 1 2

H-4.   Is *(TARGET CHILD)* the same name in which he/she appears in the school
        records or is he/she listed under a different name?

                                    The same name ....

                                    A different name (SPECIFY):........

H-5.   Why isn't *(TARGET CHILD)* enrolled in school now?   (READ ALL CATEGORIES
        AND CIRCLE AS MANY AS APPLY.)

                                    Is too young ....

        ┌──────────┐
        │ HAND   │   Is too ill or handicapped ....
        │ CARD 1 │
        └──────────┘   Dropped out ....

                                    Suspended or expelled ....

                                    Needed at home ....

                                    Went to work ....

                                    Family moved ....

                                    Other (SPECIFY): ....

H-6.   Was there something about school that led *(TARGET CHILD)* to leave
        school?   (READ ALL CATEGORIES AND CIRCLE AS MANY AS APPLY.)

                                    Disliked school ....

        ┌──────────┐
        │ HAND   │   Couldn't understand instruction in English ....
        │ CARD 2 │
        └──────────┘   Found school work too difficult ....

                                    Had to repeat too many grades ....

                                    Other (SPECIFY): ....

                                    No ....

H-7.   What is the highest grade or year of regular school *(TARGET CHILD)*
        has ever attended? (ENTER CODE IN COLUMN.)

                    20 = Never attended   07 = Seventh grade

                    21 = Prekindergarten   08 = Eighth grade

                    22 = Kindergarten   09 = Ninth grade

                    01 = First grade   10 = Tenth grade

                    02 = Second grade   11 = Eleventh grade

                    03 = Third grade   12 = Twelfth grade

                    04 = Fourth grade   13 = First year college

                    05 = Fifth grade   14 = Second year college

                    06 = Sixth grade   15 = Other (SPECIFY)

H-8.   Did *(TARGET CHILD)* complete that grade (year)?

                                    Yes ....

                                    No ....

H-4.	... 1 ... 2 _____ } (H-7)	... 1 ... 2 _____ } (H-7)	... 1 ... 2 _____ } H-7
H-5.	... 1 (H-7) ... 2 (H-7) ... 3 (H-6) ... 4 (H-7) ... 5 (H-7) ... 6 (H-7) ... 7 (H-7) ... 8 _____ (H-7)	... 1 (H-7) ... 2 (H-7) ... 3 (H-6) ... 4 (H-7) ... 5 (H-7) ... 6 (H-7) ... 7 (H-7) ... 8 _____ (H-7)	... 1 (H-7) ... 2 (H-7) ... 3 (H-6) ... 4 (H-7) ... 5 (H-7) ... 6 (H-7) ... 7 (H-7) ... 8 _____ (H-7)
H-6.	... 1 ... 2 ... 3 ... 4 ... 5 _____ _____ ... 6	... 1 ... 2 ... 3 ... 4 ... 5 _____ _____ ... 6	... 1 ... 2 ... 3 ... 4 ... 5 _____ _____ ... 6
H-7.	_____ Number	_____ Number	_____ Number
H-8.	... 1 ... 2 } (B or B)	... 1 ... 2 } (B or B)	... 1 ... 2 } (B or B)

ASK H-9 THROUGH H-12 ONLY IF *(TARGET CHILD)* WAS BORN OUTSIDE THE U.S. (REFER TO S-19). OTHERWISE, SKIP TO H-13. BE SURE TO CHECK IN BOX B.

H-9.   Did *(TARGET CHILD)* attend school before coming to the U.S.?

                           Yes ....

                           No ....

H-10.   For how many years did *(TARGET CHILD)* attend school before coming to the U.S.? (ENTER CODE IN COLUMN.)

              00 = Less than one year   08 = Eight years
              01 = One year   09 = Nine years
              02 = Two years   10 = Ten years
              03 = Three years   11 = Eleven years
              04 = Four years   12 = Twelve years
              05 = Five years   13 = Thirteen years
              06 = Six years   14 = Fourteen years
              07 = Seven years   15 = Other (SPECIFY)

H-11.   In what language was *(TARGET CHILD)* taught subjects such as arithmetic, science, and history?

                           English ....

                           Language other than English ......

H-12.   For how many years?

                           One year ....

                           Two years ....

                           Three years ....

                           Four years ....

                           Five or more years ....

H-13.   Can *(TARGET CHILD)* speak English?

                           Yes ....

                           No ....

H-14.   How well does *(TARGET CHILD)* speak English? Very well, well, not well?

                           Very well ....

                           Well (all right) ....
                                              (More than a few words)
            PROBE ────────▶ Not well {
                                              (Just a few words).....
                           Not at all ....

BOX B	☐ Born in U.S. *(H-13)* ☐ Born outside U.S.	☐ Born in U.S. *(H-13)* ☐ Born outside U.S.	☐ Born in U.S. *(H-13)* ☐ Born outside U.S.
H-9.	... 1 *(H-10)* ... 2 *(H-13)*	... 1 *(H-10)* ... 2 *(H-13)*	... 1 *(H-10)* ... 2 *(H-13)*
H-10.	_____ Number	_____ Number	_____ Number
H-11.	... 1 *(H-12)* ... 2 *(H-13)*	... 1 *(H-12)* ... 2 *(H-13)*	... 1 *(H-12)* ... 2 *(H-13)*
H-12.	... 1 ... 2 ... 3 ... 4 ... 5	... 1 ... 2 ... 3 ... 4 ... 5	... 1 ... 2 ... 3 ... 4 ... 5
H-13.	... 1 *(H-14)* ... 2 *(H-15)*	... 1 *(H-14)* ... 2 *(H-15)*	... 1 *(H-14)* ... 2 *(H-15)*
H-14.	... 1 ... 2 ... 3 ... 4 ... 5	... 1 ... 2 ... 3 ... 4 ... 5	... 1 ... 2 ... 3 ... 4 ... 5

H-15.   Can *(TARGET CHILD)* understand spoken English?

                              Yes ....

                              No ....

H-16.   How well does *(TARGET CHILD)* understand spoken English? Very well,
         well, not well?

                              Very well ....

                              Well (all right) ....
                                             ((More than a few words)
                    PROBE ──➤ Not well {
                                             ((Just a few words).....
                              Not at all ....

H-17.   Can *(TARGET CHILD)* read and write English?

                              Yes ....

                              No ....

H-13.   How well does *(TARGET CHILD)* read and write English? Very well,
         well, not well?

                              Very well ....

                              Well (all right) ....
                                             ((More than a few words)
                    PROBE ──➤ Not well {
                                             ((Just a few words).....
                              Not at all ....

H-15.	... 1 *(H-16)*	... 1 *(H-16)*	... 1 *(H-16)*
	... 2 *(H-17)*	... 2 *(H-17)*	... 2 *(H-17)*
H-16.	... 1	... 1	... 1
	... 2	... 2	... 2
	... 3	... 3	... 3
	... 4	... 4	... 4
	... 5	... 5	... 5
H-17.	... 1 *(H-16)*	... 1 *(H-18)*	... 1 *(H-18)*
	... 2 *(Box C)*	... 2 *(Box C)*	... 2 *(Box C)*
H-18.	... 1	... 1	... 1
	... 2	... 2	... 2
	... 3 } *(Box C)*	... 3 } *(Box C)*	... 3 } *(Box C)*
	... 4	... 4	... 4
	... 5	... 5	... 5

```
┌─────────────────────────────────────────────────────────────────────────┐
│                              ┌──────────┐                                 │
│                              │  BOX C   │                                 │
│                              └──────────┘                                 │
│                                                                           │
│  IN H-19 THROUGH H-22, NON-ENGLISH HOME LANGUAGE REFERS TO THE NON-ENGLISH LANGUAGE │
│  THAT IS USUALLY OR OFTEN SPOKEN BY THE PEOPLE IN THE HOUSEHOLD (REFER TO S-2 AND    │
│  S-3 ON THE SCREENER).  IF THE RESPONSES TO BOTH S-2 AND S-3 ARE NON-ENGLISH LANGUAGES │
│  ASK ABOUT S-2, THE LANGUAGE USUALLY SPOKEN.  BE SURE TO ENTER THIS LANGUAGE IN BOX C. │
├─────────────────────────────────────────────────────────────────────────┤
```

H-19.   Can *(TARGET CHILD)* speak and understand spoken *(NON-ENGLISH HOME LANGUAGE)*?

                           Yes ....

                           No ....

H-20.   How well does *(TARGET CHILD)* speak and understand spoken *(NON-ENGLISH HOME LANGUAGE)*? Very well, well, not well?

                           Very well ....

                           Well (all right) ....
                                                  (More than a few words)
             PROBE ──────▶ Not well {
                                                  (Just a few words).....
                           Not at all......................

H-21.   Can *(TARGET CHILD)* read and write *(NON-ENGLISH HOME LANGUAGE)*?

                           Yes ....

                           No ....

H-22.   How well does *(TARGET CHILD)* read and write *(NON-ENGLISH HOME LANGUAGE)*? Very well, well, not well?

                           Very well ....

                           Well (all right) ....
                                                  (More than a few words)
             PROBE ──────▶ Not well {
                                                  (Just a few words).....
                           Not at all ....

BOX C	NON-ENGLISH HOME LANGUAGE		
H-19.	... 1 (H-20) ... 2 (H-21)	... 1 (H-20) ... 2 (H-21)	... 1 (H-20) ... 2 (H-21)
H-20.	... 1 ... 2 ... 3 ... 4 ... 5	... 1 ... 2 ... 3 ... 4 ... 5	... 1 ... 2 ... 3 ... 4 ... 5
H-21.	... 1 (H-22) ... 2 (Box D)	... 1 (H-22) ... 2 (Box D)	... 1 (H-22) ... 2 (Box D)
H-22.	... 1 ... 2 ... 3 } (Box D) ... 4 ... 5	... 1 ... 2 ... 3 } (Box D) ... 4 ... 5	... 1 ... 2 ... 3 } (Box D) ... 4 ... 5

ASK H-23 ONLY IF *(TARGET CHILD)* HAS BROTHERS OR SISTERS (REFER TO S-11).
OTHERWISE, SKIP TO H-24. BE SURE TO CHECK IN BOX D.

H-23.   What language does *(TARGET CHILD)* usually speak to his/her brothers
         and sisters? (ENTER CODE IN COLUMN.)

HAND
CARD 3

01 = English	11 = Navajo
02 = Arabic	12 = Polish
03 = Chinese	13 = Portuguese
04 = Filipino (Tagalog, Ilocano)	14 = Russian
05 = French	15 = Scandinavian language
06 = German	16 = Spanish
07 = Greek	17 = Vietnamese
08 = Italian	18 = Yiddish
09 = Japanese	19 = Other (SPECIFY)
10 = Korean	

H-24   What language does *(TARGET CHILD)* usually speak to his/her best
        friends? (ENTER CODE IN COLUMN.)

HAND
CARD 3

01 = English	11 = Navajo
02 = Arabic	12 = Polish
03 = Chinese	13 = Portuguese
04 = Filipino (Tagalog, Ilocano)	14 = Russian
05 = French	15 = Scandinavian language
06 = German	16 = Spanish
07 = Greek	17 = Vietnamese
08 = Italian	18 = Yiddish
09 = Japanese	19 = Other (SPECIFY)
10 = Korean	20 = Don't know

BOX D	☐ Has brothers or sisters ☐ Does **not** have brothers or sisters *(H-24)*	☐ Has brothers or sisters ☐ Does **not** have brothers or sisters *(H-24)*	☐ Has brothers or sisters ☐ Does **not** have brothers or sisters *(H-24)*
H-23.	_____ Number	_____ Number	_____ Number
H-24.	_____ *(Box E)* Number	_____ *(Box E)* Number	_____ *(Box E)* Number

BEFORE ASKING H-25 THROUGH H-32, REFER TO H-1.

- IF (TARGET CHILD) IS CURRENTLY ENROLLED IN OR ATTENDING SCHOOL, SAY:

  As I told you, we will be going to (TARGET CHILD'S) school to find out
  what he/she is being taught in school, but now I would like to know if
  (TARGET CHILD) is receiving any instruction in <u>English</u> from anywhere
  besides a regular school?

  Yes ....

  No ....

- IF (TARGET CHILD) IS NOT CURRENTLY ENROLLED IN OR ATTENDING SCHOOL, SAY:

  Now I would like to know if (TARGET CHILD) is receiving any instruction
  in <u>English</u> from anywhere besides a regular school?

  Yes ....

  No ....

H-25. What is (TARGET CHILD) being taught to do in English? (READ EACH
CATEGORY AND CIRCLE YES OR NO FOR EACH.)

| HAND CARD 4 |

To speak the language better ....

To understand the spoken language better ....

To read the language better ....

To write the language better ....

Mathematics ....

Science ....

Social Studies ....

Other (SPECIFY): ....

H-26 Who is teaching it? (READ ALL CATEGORIES AND CIRCLE AS MANY AS APPLY.)

| HAND CARD 5 |

Mother, father, sister, or brother of (TARGET CHILD).......

Another relative or a friend or acquaintance ....

Teacher ....

Private, paid tutor ....

Other (SPECIFY) ....

BOX E			
	☐ Enrolled in school ... 1*(H-25)* ... 2*(H-28)* ☐ <u>Not</u> enrolled <u>in</u> school ... 1*(H-25)* ... 2*(H-28)*	☐ Enrolled in school ... 1*(H-25)* ... 2*(H-28)* ☐ <u>Not</u> enrolled <u>in</u> school ... 1*(H-25)* ... 2*(H-28)*	☐ Enrolled in school ... 1*(H-25)* ... 2*(H-28)* ☐ <u>Not</u> enrolled <u>in</u> school ... 1*(H-25)* ... 2*(H-28)*

H-25	<u>Yes</u> <u>No</u>	<u>Yes</u> <u>No</u>	<u>Yes</u> <u>No</u>
	1 2	1 2	1 2
	1 2	1 2	1 2
	1 2	1 2	1 2
	1 2	1 2	1 2
	1 2	1 2	1 2
	1 2	1 2	1 2
	1 2	1 2	1 2
	_____	_____	_____

H-26.			
	... 1 ... 2 ... 3 ... 4 ... 5 _____ _____	... 1 ... 2 ... 3 ... 4 ... 5 _____ _____	... 1 ... 2 ... 3 ... 4 ... 5 _____ _____

H-27. **Where is it being taught?** (READ ALL CATEGORIES AND CIRCLE AS MANY AS APPLY.)

> In a church building ....
>
> ┌──────┐
> │ HAND │ In a community organization or social service agency
> │ CARD │ (YMCA, etc.) ....
> │ 6   │
> └──────┘ In a school building ....
>
> In the home of *(TARGET CHILD)*, a friend, relative or tutor.
>
> Other (SPECIFY)..

H-28. **Is *(TARGET CHILD)* receiving any instruction in <u>any language</u> <u>other</u> <u>than English</u> from anywhere besides a regular school?**

> Yes ....
>
> No ....

H-29. **In what language?** (ENTER CODE IN COLUMN.)

┌──────────┐
│ HAND   │
│ CARD 3 │
└──────────┘

02 = Arabic	11 = Navajo
03 = Chinese	12 = Polish
04 = Filipino (Tagalog, Ilocano)	13 = Portuguese
05 = French	14 = Russian
06 = German	15 = Scandinavian language
07 = Greek	16 = Spanish
08 = Italian	17 = Vietnamese
09 = Japanese	18 = Yiddish
10 = Korean	19 = Other (SPECIFY)

81

H-27.			
	... 1	... 1	... 1
	... 2	... 2	... 2
	... 3	... 3	... 3
	... 4	... 4	... 4
	... 5 _____	... 5 _____	... 5 _____
	_____	_____	_____
H-28.	... 1 *(H-29)*	... 1 *(H-29)*	... 1 *(H-29)*
	... 2 *(Box F)*	... 2 *(Box F)*	... 2 *(Box F)*
H-29.	_____ Number	_____ Number	_____ Number

H-30.   What is (TARGET CHILD) being taught to do in (LANGUAGE)?   (READ EACH
        CATEGORY AND CIRCLE YES OR NO FOR EACH.)

        ┌──────────┐   To speak the language better ....
        │ HAND   │   To understand the spoken language better ....
        │ CARD 4 │   To read the language better ....
        └──────────┘   To write the language better ....
                         Mathematics ....
                         Science ....
                         Social Studies ....
                         Other (SPECIFY): ....

H-31.   Who is teaching it? (READ ALL CATEGORIES AND CIRCLE AS MANY AS APPLY.)

        ┌──────────┐   Mother, father, sister, or brother of
        │ HAND   │   (TARGET CHILD) ....
        │ CARD 5 │   Another relative or a friend or acquaintance ....
        └──────────┘   Teacher ....
                         Private, paid tutor ....
                         Other (SPECIFY):....................................

H-32.   Where is it being taught?   (READ ALL CATEGORIES AND CIRCLE AS MANY AS
        APPLY.)

        ┌──────────┐   In a church building ....
        │ HAND   │   In a community organization or social service agency
        │ CARD 6 │   (YMCA, etc.) ....
        └──────────┘   In a school building ....
                         In the home of (TARGET CHILD), a friend, relative,
                         or tutor ....
                         Other (SPECIFY):....................................

┌─────────┐
│ BOX F │
└─────────┘

IF MORE THAN ONE TARGET CHILD, GO BACK TO H-1 ON PAGE 1.   OTHERWISE, GO TO H-33.

	TARGET CHILD 1	TARGET CHILD 2	TARGET CHILD 3
	Last name:	Last name:	Last name:
	- - - - - - - - -	- - - - - - - - -	- - - - - - - -
	First name:	First name:	First name:
	Age:_____	Age:_____	Age:_____

	TARGET CHILD 1		TARGET CHILD 2		TARGET CHILD 3	
	Yes	No	Yes	No	Yes	No
H-30.	1	2	1	2	1	2
	1	2	1	2	1	2
	1	2	1	2	1	2
	1	2	1	2	1	2
	1	2	1	2	1	2
	1	2	1	2	1	2
	1	2	1	2	1	2
	1	2	1	2	1	2
	_____		_____		_____	

H-31.			
	... 1	... 1	... 1
	... 2	... 2	... 2
	... 3	... 3	... 3
	... 4	... 4	... 4
	... 5 _____	... 5 _____	... 5 _____
	_____	_____	_____
	_____	_____	_____

H-32.			
	... 1	... 1	... 1
	... 2 } Box F	... 2 } Box F	... 2 } Box F
	... 3	... 3	... 3
	... 4	... 4	... 4
	... 5 _____	... 5 _____	... 5 _____
	_____	_____	_____

APPENDIX   E

LANGUAGES SPOKEN BY INTERVIEWERS

Table E - 1

Bilingualism Among Field Staff

Language	Total	Coordinators and Regional Supervisors	Assistant Field Supervisors	Interviewer	Test Administrators	Trouble Shooters
English Only	181	8	8	104	54	7
Bilingual						
French	2			2		
German	3			3		
Hebrew	1			1		
Italian	3			3		
Japanese	3			3		
Navajo	1			1		
Norwegian	1			1		
Polish	1			1		
Portuguese	1			1		
Spanish	91	4		65	19	3
Yiddish	7			7		
Bilingual Total	114	4		88	19	3

NOTES

1. Retrieval of CESS data tapes and accompanying documentation is being arranged through the following sources: Reference Service Machine Readable Archives Division—NNR, National Archives and Records Service, Washington, D.C. 20408 (telephone 202/724-1080); and Inter-University Consortium for Political and Social Research, P.O. Box 1248, Ann Arbor, Mich. 48106.

2. D. Dubois, *The Children's English and Services Study: A Methodological Review* (Washington, D.C.: National Center for Educational Statistics, 1980).

3. Ibid., p. 8.

4. Ibid., p. 15.

5. L. Rudner, R. Sitgreaves, and J. Chambers, *Reanalysis of the Number of Limited English Proficient Students Estimated in the Children's English and Services Study* (Washington, D.C.: National Institute of Education, 1981).

6. Since the writing of this report, a decision has been rendered in favor of the plaintiffs.

REFERENCES

The educational disadvantage of language minority persons in the United States, Spring 1974. National Center for Education Statistics (NCES) Bulletin 78 B-4, Department of Health, Education, and Welfare, 1978a.

Geographic distribution, nativity, and age distribution of language minorities in the United States: Spring 1976. National Center for Education Statistics (NCES) Bulletin 78 B-5, Department of Health, Education, and Welfare, 1978b.

Place of birth and language characteristics of persons of Hispanic origin in the United States, Spring 1976. National Center for Education Statistics (NCES) Bulletin 78 B-5, Department of Health, Education, and Welfare, 1978c.

Birthplace and language characteristics of persons of Chinese, Japanese, Korean, Philipino, and Vietnamese Origin in the United States, Spring 1976. National Center for Education Statistics (NCES) Bulletin 79 B-12, Department of Health, Education, and Welfare, May 1979.